He Laid His Hand Upon Me

Luke Weaver

Copyright © 2001 Luke Weaver

ISBN 1-931600-03-1

Unless noted otherwise, the scriptures quoted in this book were taken from the King James Version of the Bible. In the case where other translations were easier to understand, either the New King James (NKJ) or the New Living Translation (NLT) was used.

Printed in the United States of America

DEDICATION

I dedicate this book to my precious wife, Edna, who has been faithful to me; and to my children who encouraged me in writing my life story.

With our children in 2000…

…and some of our grandchildren.

ACKNOWLEDGMENT

Mary and Victor Stutzman

I thank Victor and Mary Stutzman for their many hours they so cheerfully gave to help me "cross this mountain" as Victor typed most of the book on the computer and Mary worked diligently on the editing.

Thank you, Barry Hutchens, for supplying the reams of paper.

Thanks to Joanne Derstine Hellier, Bob Armstrong, Ann and Vern Hartley and Shelly Tison for encouraging me by contributing their expertise.

Thanks to Nathan Weaver, my grandson, who is on the cover photo.

Thanks to Josiah Maust, my grandson, for his excellent cover design.

CONTENTS

FOREWORD

From the first time that my life came into contact with Luke and Edna Weaver, I sensed the hand of God upon this man's life. We were destined to be friends throughout our lifetime. Our backgrounds were similar, being reared in Pennsylvania Mennonite homes.

Immediately, I saw a passion for God when I had my first conversation with this precious couple. To my wife, Beulah, and me, we consider it an honor to be close friends with Luke and Edna Weaver. You will pick up quickly the honesty, purity and simplicity which flows so freely from these committed lives.

Your life will also be challenged as you read the contents of this book. Luke had one thing only in mind, that is to glorify God. If you have never met Luke and Edna, you will have an intense desire to meet this family after reading how God has been with and led their lives through difficult and also challenging circumstances.

There seem to be few men who make a commitment and can follow through. Luke is a man of his word. He will stand behind his word and inspiration is the result. We have worked side by side for many years, including having a part in his establishing a great church in the Harrisburg and Elizabethtown area of Pennsylvania, his home country.

You will be fascinated with Luke's story in this book. You will want to share this book with your children and friends. Today, Luke and Edna are co-workers with my son, Phil Derstine, Senior Pastor of Florida Christian Retreat Family Church. Allow God to bless you as Luke shares his life with you in this book.

Gerald G. Derstine, D.D.
Chairman, Gospel Crusade, Inc.
President, Strawberry Lake Christian Retreat Church, Inc.
Founder-Director, Israel Affairs International

FOREWORD (Continued)

Pastors Luke and Edna Weaver are ordinary people who have lived extraordinary lives. This book is more than an autobiography of significant events. Rather, it is a road map to the making of a legacy and a living testimony of the faithfulness of God to His trusted servants.

Our families grew up together. Forged in the fires of spiritual renewal, we shared a Mennonite heritage and an insatiable hunger for more of God. The Derstines and the Weavers encouraged each other through the uncharted waters of change, rocking the boat of life-long Mennonite tradition.

Today, Jannette and I are blessed to have Luke and Edna serving by our side at Christian Retreat Family Church, adding the wisdom of years of experience to our ministry staff. The integrity of their lives is further accented by their attentiveness to the needs of others. They are the first to respond to crisis needs in the church, seemingly unaffected by early mornings or late, long hours.

Energized by a divine ministry call, their legacy continues and the living line-up of fruit that remains continues to grow. Read their story carefully. Give particular attention to the values of honesty, simplicity, and integrity that they live by. Allow your life to enter the realm of the extraordinary through greater surrender to the leadership of the Holy Spirit!

Pastors Phil & Jannette Derstine
Christian Retreat Family Church
Bradenton, Florida

FOREWORD (Continued)

Luke and Edna Weaver are parents and pioneers to many of us. They have forged a spiritual trail in our region of Pennsylvania that has become a highway for the glory of God. At a time when many churches were ignorant of or unwilling to press into the ministry of the Holy Spirit, Luke and Edna were plunging in. They resisted pressures to conform. They refused to compromise. They were willing to make mistakes and learn from them.

They taught us to love Jesus. They taught us to hold nothing back from the One who holds nothing back. We learned to soar in worship and persevere in prayer. They taught us with more than words. Their lives spoke the message.

We are seeing the abundant fruit of their devotion. For years Edna faithfully went to the state Capitol building in Harrisburg. She tirelessly cried out for God to move in the hearts of state legislators. Recently, a dear Christian senator requested that pastors from the region join him in his office weekly for prayer. In addition, a number of other senators have requested a time of receiving prayer ministry from local pastors. Also, in a few months, Pennsylvania will become the second state in the U.S. to install a full-time, born again chaplain to minister to state leaders.

Luke's familiar cry, "Glory!", is also being fulfilled. Currently, over 150 pastors in our region have committed to praying together and serving together on a regular basis. Many churches throughout the area are beginning to receive a revelation of God's glory. Churches are committing to 24-hour prayer. The Holy Spirit is welcomed in churches and circles that would have resisted Him years ago. A passionate spirit of worship is arising among us. There is an increasing number of people getting saved and baptized in the Spirit. Pastors want God. People are thirsty for Him.

Luke and Edna, along with other diligent parents and pioneers, are receiving fruit from their labors of love.

I personally have been powerfully touched by their faithfulness to Jesus. As a young man in the 1970's, I sensed a call of God on my life. I also fought with a tremendous bondage to fear. Luke ministered mighty grace to me. I saw the clutches of terror and intimidation broken from my life as he prayed for me and walked with me. I am so grateful for this spiritual father who fought for my freedom. The fruit of his ministry has lasted.

Only heaven will fully tell the fruit of any life. Yet, glimpses of fruit help us this side of heaven. Luke and Edna, I hope that words from those whom your lives have touched will give you a foretaste of the Father's, "Well done!"

Thank you for being faithful. You are fearless pioneers...and faithful parents. Glory!!!

Pastor David Hess
Pastor of Christ Community Church
Camp Hill, Pennsylvania

FOREWORD (Continued)

Papa Luke and Mamma Luke (Edna): This is how most of us of the Haitian people and children call them. Reverend and Mrs. Luke Weaver have become like our adoptive Haitian parents. For more than 25 years now they have dedicated their lives to help make a difference in the nation of Haiti as well as in many other countries of the world.

In January 1973 with the help of Reverend Gerald Derstine and Leslie and Fern Helman, my wife, Doris, (19 years old then) and I (25) came to visit the United States for the first time. While we were both still under culture shock, seeing things like automatic sliding doors, escalators, bridges, overpasses and countless other things, we were sitting down at Christian Retreat Cafeteria in Bradenton, Florida, when a man with a big smile walked up to our table and handed us some money. I learned later that this man was Pastor Luke Weaver. A few weeks later we were invited to his church on Derry Street in Harrisburg, Pennsylvania. There we made acquaintance with his ministry and family. On a visit to Haiti, Pastor Luke felt touched by the great need in my small church and school that had just started. He went back to his church in Pennsylvania and asked his people to start supporting our work. So he became seriously involved in financially assisting our school teachers, the feeding program for the children, the sewing and home economics school, our pastors from the mountain, and even the construction of our church, Grace Tabernacle, and our two story school building. Grace Chapel contributed in purchasing the land for the school building, the missionary house, and for the ministry, a nice brand new fourteen foot bed diesel truck that lasted fifteen years. Grace Chapel sent and helped to support Carl and Jean Shelly who spent four years with us in Haiti to help build the work and supervise the Gospel Crusade Churches and schools. Pastor Luke encouraged his daughter Irene Weaver to spend three months with us in Haiti to help with the administration. On every trip, many candies were brought to the children and neckties were given to the pastors who attended the annual convention and pastors' seminars taught by Pastor Luke himself. It did not take long until the children changed his name to "Papa Luke" and Edna to "Mamma Luke." Pretty soon the Haitian pastors as well as the members began to call the reverend "papa" as a sign of respect, gratitude and love.

My family has become part of the Weaver family. My wife and I have spent over three months in their home on Faith Circle, Blue Mountain in Harrisburg, where my wife delivered our second son, Joel-Helman. We will never forget how Papa Luke turned Irene's little Pontiac into an ambulance and how he rushed my wife to the Harrisburg Hospital. Red traffic lights could not be respected, because her water already broke and her labor pains had begun.

God used Papa and Mamma Luke so many times to bring miracles to our life and to the work in Haiti. Our first little new Lada Niva car was a miracle from God given to us through Papa Luke and Pastor Melvin Weaver in 1986. Then again in 1990, out of his own pocket Papa Luke made the first contribution towards the purchase of our new Isuzu Trooper. Then he asked his cousin Bill Martin to have his bank buy the vehicle for us while he arranged the payments to be made by Grace Chapel and Christ Community Church at Camp Hill, Pennsylvania.

Truly Reverend Luke and Edna are like real parents to us. All of their children and grandchildren treat us as brothers and sisters, uncles and aunts. I had the honor to travel to Ivory Coast, Africa, with Papa and Mamma Luke, their son, Luke, Jr. and his wife, Bonnie. I was blessed to see Papa Luke ordained as a Bishop over the nations as he was already a Bishop over Haiti. The great love he has in his life for the nations explains why God would choose him to bless the nations. I have not yet met any one on this planet who sincerely loves people greater than Papa Luke. He is one of the rare people in whose presence you do not feel the complexity or the barriers of nationality, color, or background differences. You cannot help but feel the respect, equality, honesty, sincere love and God's very presence in him.

It would take many pages to write about this man and his family. However, I would like to encourage anyone who has the blessed privilege to meet Papa Luke or to read the testimonies of his life experience with God in his book *He Laid His Hand Upon Me*, to seize the opportunity. I know many blessings will be received even as my family and I have been blessed.

Papa Luke, you are a special gift from heaven! Your life and ministry have been a pattern for me. Through your encouragement, my testimony of physical resurrection has now been heard around the world. It has made a way for me in high places and it keeps opening new doors for my ministry around the world. By the way, I am writing this foreword in Oakridge on the small island of Roatan, Honduras while all preparations have been already made for me and my team to minister in Germany in a couple of weeks from now. Thanks for your encouragement! You advised me not to leave Haiti at a time when it was very tough for us. Now the Lord is using me to change the history of my nation and to bring the whole country under the leadership of God, "One nation under God." I am so thankful that I didn't leave Haiti.

May your life continue to be a powerful lighthouse to guide the young leaders on their way to excelling in their endeavor to fulfill God's call on their lives. May the reading of *He Laid His Hand Upon Me* help them find the direction to success with God as they learn the secret of total commitment and surrender. May "His Hand" on you continue to touch many more lives in all the nations you are called to until Jesus comes. Glory!

Bishop Joel R. Jeune
International Coordinator, Gospel Crusade of Haiti
Host, TBN Haitian Praise The Lord International Coordinator
Christian Movement For A New Haiti President
Grace International, Inc.

FOREWORD (Continued)

Sherlyn and I became acquainted with Luke and Edna Weaver in 1974 when we were searching for more of the power of God. Luke and Edna taught at a Bible study we were attending in Southern Lancaster County, Pennsylvania. They helped us understand and move into the fullness of the Holy Spirit. Their love for Jesus and their desire to help people be filled with the Holy Spirit was and is an inspiration to many. Because of their input into our lives, we have great respect for them. We thank God for the example they have been to us in ministry and in living lives that glorify God. We value Luke and Edna's friendship and love them dearly.

Pastor Sam and Sherlyn Smucker
Worship Center
Lancaster, Pennsylvania

This book provides not only an insightful experience of the unique culture of a Pennsylvania Dutch Mennonite community in the early 1900's but also an opportunity of having your faith increased and your life being refreshed and renewed in the things of the Lord. You will see how the hand of God was upon a little boy who grew up in a Pennsylvania Dutch farming community in the 1920's and 30's and who became a mighty man of great faith. You will also discover how he and his beloved wife, Edna, impacted the government of Pennsylvania as well as many other parts of the world, including the nation of Haiti, with the simple love and power of the Holy Spirit.

Victor Stutzman

INTRODUCTION
He Laid His Hand Upon Me

I believe that God called me from my mother's womb just as the Prophet Jeremiah was called of God according to Jeremiah 1:4 & 5. When the Lord baptized me with the Holy Spirit in August of 1957, He laid His hand upon me. I physically felt a hand laid upon my head that day. Revelation 1:17b says "And He laid His right hand upon me." His presence was so precious that I recognized the hand of God on my life many times just as the psalmist described his experience in Psalm 139:5 "and laid Your hand upon me." NKJ

This promise is to you when you are born again. As you read this book, you will have the blessing of God imparted to you and He will give you new strength. Jesus said in Acts 1:8 "But ye shall receive power, after that the Holy Ghost is come upon you: and ye shall be witnesses unto Me both in Jerusalem, and in all Judea, and in Samaria, and unto the uttermost part of the earth."

At the time of this writing, I am serving as associate pastor with Pastor Phil Derstine at Christian Retreat Family Church and Edna and I are living in the church parsonage. I am also the Area Coordinator of Southwest Florida for Gospel Crusade Ministerial Fellowship.

The purpose of this book, He Laid His Hand Upon Me:

Because God laid His Hand upon me, the Lord has a special call on my life, and this book could be called "Touching Incidents and Remarkable Answers to Prayer." My desire is that this book will be a tool to win many souls to our Lord Jesus, and that many will receive the fullness of the Holy Spirit. And we pray that many believers will come into a deeper relationship with our Lord Jesus.

The motto of my life is found in two scriptures: Proverbs 4:18 "But the path of the just is as the shining light, that shineth more and more unto the perfect day." I Corinthians 15:57 and 58 "But thanks be to God, which giveth us the victory through our Lord Jesus Christ. Therefore, my beloved brethren, be ye stedfast, unmoveable, always abounding in the work of the Lord, forasmuch as ye know that your labour is not in vain in the Lord."

CHAPTER 1
MY CHILDHOOD

*D. O. Weaver, my father, with the harvest team in
North Dakota in 1915 before he was married.*

February 20th, 1926

It was a cold sunny day on February 20th, 1926 when David
and Lizzie Martin Weaver became parents of their sixth child
on my sister Edna's seventh birthday. Edna was the "big girl
helper" for Mam Lizzie around the house.

My folks lived on Grandma Martin's farm in Weaverland. One
of my early memories was that I could still walk under the
kitchen table standing tall and also taking the little wooden
bobsled down the hill on our driveway at the age of three. I
also remember playing on the Titan 10-20 tractor parked in
the tractor shed and, at another time, losing the tip of my left
index finger when I accidentally caught it in the shaker
contraption of the two-hole corn sheller. Mam was the nurse
again and she scolded big brother John, about five or six years
old, for not being more careful watching out for the little
ones.

The Big Bulldog Mack Truck

The big Bulldog, a Mack Truck, had hard rubber tires and a heavy chain drive fastened to the rear wheels and an open cab making it look like quite a monster of a truck. Pap used it to work in the fields. He hauled walnut logs to the Bowertown casket factory. This old truck also had a whistle used as a horn. Since the cab was open and not closed in to keep the cold air out, Pap had to buy a sheepskin coat to keep warm while driving.

Well, Grandma Martin did not think too much of having a son-in-law as a truck driver. I guess that was why years later Mam told me that Grandma did not think much of Pap's worldly sheepskin coat. You see, D. O. (my Dad) was what you would call a contemporary, today. He was one of the first to buy a car. Well, the tension got so bad that it split the church in 1927. Bishop Joe Wenger headed up the conservative group, the Groffdale Conference, which kept using the horse and buggies and Bishop Moses Horning headed up the liberals, the Weaverland Conference, which believed that you could own or have a car and still be a Christian.

Dark Days of Gloom

At the age of four, I came down with pneumonia which grew worse instead of better. The fever stayed high and I needed constant care. Finally Dr. Wenger, our local family doctor from Terre Hill about one and a half miles away, decided that the only way to save my life was to operate on my right lung which had developed a very large pus sack that was about to kill me. Dr. Wenger brought his nurse along and proceeded with the operation on the kitchen table. The anesthesia that he gave me was not sufficient because I was awakened about half way through this massive butcher type operation. It took both the nurse and my father to hold me down while the doctor cut through one rib to make ample room for the drainage. I was so sick that I only remembered them changing my chest bandages. They used old pieces of clean strips of cloths to replace my bandages while I was in recovery from the operation. I can still remember looking down at my right side under my arm and noticing the large rubber tube endings sticking out and fastened by a large safety pin. This device was kept there for many days so that all the drainage could be soaked up by the bandages that were changed regularly.

One other thing that I remember about my recovery was one night when Uncle Sam Martin (my mother's brother) spent the night with me. It was the time of year when the farmers were sterilizing the tobacco seedbeds with steam pressure. They changed the steam pans every 20 minutes. Whenever the 20 minutes were up, the steam whistle would blow. During that one particular night while my uncle stayed by my bedside to keep my mind off my discomfort, he and I were entertained by this steam whistle sounding outside next to my bedroom. I guess I was Uncle Sam's favorite little nephew. He called me Lukie Boy.

Well, through tender, loving care and the silent prayers of the faith of my parents and many relatives and friends of the family, I slowly but surely recovered. As Jeremiah was called to be a prophet from his mother's womb (Jer.1:4 - 8), so was I called from my mother's womb to be a minister of the Gospel as noted in the introduction of this book.

Moving Day

April 1, 1930 arrived and the moving day was started by an early rising. The furniture and all of our other possessions were transported to a new community across the Ephrata Mountain just northeast of Ephrata, Pennsylvania on the Johnny Weaver Farm (Edna's Great Uncle.) Now this move took place only about six weeks after my operation. Even though our church allowed us to have cars, we were restricted to using only the touring cars. It would have been too cold in Pap's "Baby Grand Touring Chevy" to take me on the long twelve mile journey to our new home across the mountain. So our neighbor, Aaron Snader, Sr. offered to take me in his Model T Ford sedan which was probably a 1926 model. By now I was responding well; yet I had to take great caution so that I would not have a relapse. That was before the days of miracle drugs. My illness left me with a double curvature of the spine and the therapy prescribed was to put two big nails on both sides of the pump house door and a broom stick across the door just above my reach. To straighten up my back, I was to hang from this broom stick everyday without my feet touching the floor. Praise God, it worked!

The Johnny Weaver Farm

It seemed that everyone adjusted quickly while living in the new community. It was exciting to me to explore the large barn and the largest tobacco shed I had ever seen. My

The house where I was born.

brother, John, and I would explore every place, climbing onto the top of the tobacco shed and then on up as high into the barn as possible. At the ages of six and seven, we ventured into many dangerous places. John and I were close buddies, but there were times when we would get into a quarrel with each other. My oldest brother, Rufus, would then take my side and I would feel secure, all of this only to be quickly forgotten.

Pap bought baby chicks and put them under the warm canopy of the brooder stove in the round brooder house. Billy Hastler, my neighbor buddy, often came to play with me. One day we had the greatest fun in taking Pap's chick feed and putting it out on the floor where we played, pretending the feed to be sand. Well, the fun ended after Pap came in from the brooder house that night. I don't remember what Pap said, but I do remember getting a good sound spanking. Well, that was the first of my two whippings I got from Pap. Somehow I don't remember how many Mam gave me.

Springville Church

We went to Springville Church every two weeks. It was there that I sat with Adam Weaver and Melvin High. I remember Bishop Joe Hostetter. He would usually start out with Luke 10:5 which declares "'Peace be to this House.' It is my desire to have the Peace of God rest upon us in this morning service." This was spoken in the German. I liked it when Bishop Joe Hostetter spoke because he did not preach as long as the rest of the preachers. I also knew he spoke very meaningfully. We were there to help build the new Springville Church in 1938.

A Rainy Day

It was on a rainy day when Rufus was directed to clear out the wagon shed which also housed the corn cribs. Once the spring wagon was loaded with dirt and corn cobs, Rufus hitched Bill (the lead horse) to the wagon. I sat on top of the load while it was being delivered down to the Cocalico Creek embankment. In order to get close to the bank to unload the wagon, Rufus tried to back the wagon up against a big stump. This was done so that when he would open the tail gate, the dirt would fall down easily onto the embankment. But when Bill started backing up, the strength of this heavy horse was too powerful to stop in time to avoid crashing the left rear wheel into the stump. As a result, the spring wagon suddenly went completely down over the bank throwing me off the wagon. I was scared and as I was scrambling for safety I fell into the creek. The broken wheel was replaced by another wheel just a little smaller which was manageable.

To Grandfather's House We Go

Grandfather John B. and Grandmother Anna Weaver lived in Juniata County, Pennsylvania. They became restless and were looking for new territory. So in the spring of 1900 when Pap was six years old, Grandpa (or Grossdaughty which was Pennsylvania Dutch for grandfather) moved his family from Mexico, Pennsylvania near Mifflintown to Lancaster County. They moved by loading their possessions on the train at Thompsontown, Pennsylvania. Grandpa settled down in Bareville on Schule Haus Wage (Pennsylvania Dutch for School House Road) next to Good's one room schoolhouse.

It was a Sunday afternoon and Pap and Mam decided to visit Grandpa and Grandma Weaver. We were always excited about going there. It was so refreshing to visit Grandparents John and Anna. Their kindness and sweetness were outstanding. Their buildings were always well-kept and clean, their garden always kept neat with no weeds to be found, and their yard was always mowed and trimmed on time. Grandpa John Weaver was a man of few words, but his smiles and little chuckles of laughter were so pleasant. Grandma Weaver seemed to always have those big white or pink candy lozenges. Her cooking was outstanding.

Whenever we visited Grandpa's farm, I would help with

the chores. On one occasion we were getting one of the large strawbales to bed the cows when one of my brothers, John, took the bale hook and thrust it into the straw. When I pushed the strawbale, the hook accidentally slipped out of the straw causing John to plunge onto the concrete about 12 feet below. He broke his arm and was taken to the doctor to have a splint and bandage put on his arm. He was then ordered to keep his arm bandaged for about six weeks and was excused from the chores until his arm was healed.

There were times that Grandpa and Grandma Weaver would come in their horse and carriage to our house for dinner which meant that they would have to drive twelve miles from their house to ours. When the church split in 1927, he decided to stay with the Groffdale Conference. Only in the case of emergency would he ride in an auto. We always knew him to be a man of conviction. So they had to start the long trip to our house soon after seven in the morning and would arrive at our house about a half an hour before noon. It was a great day to have them visit us.

One time Grandpa told us how he was kneeling down and fixing the fence at the field by the road when a neighbor came along and said, "John, are you praying?" and he replied, "We all should do more of that."

The Depression Years

I was three years old in 1929 when the stock market collapsed and the Great Depression fell upon the good old U.S.A. We were poor but I didn't know it. There always was food on the table. We had beef and pork, plenty of milk and chickens to produce the eggs. We also had vegetables from the garden and potatoes from the field and lots of home canned vegetables and fruit.

We took wheat to the feedmill to have it ground to flour. We bought salt in 100 pound bags at the feed mill and it was used for table salt and for cattle salt. We roasted ear corn and shelled and ground it for corn meal. We cooked it, and oh, it was good! — hot corn meal mush and milk with some salt sprinkled on it. The left over was put in a pan and cut up when it was cold. Then for breakfast we made this leftover into fried mush and pudding, which is scraps of meat cooked for mush toppings. Then to top it off, we put some homemade ketchup and a bit of onions on top of it. We also had scrapple which was meat scraps mixed with corn meal. There just wasn't much money around.

I remember in the early 1930's when the depression was upon our nation that there was very little money for groceries. So before I went to bed at night it was my assigned task to grind the wheat which was raised on the farm to toast it in the oven for breakfast the next morning. We had an old coffee grinder which I used for that purpose, and I got tired of eating whole wheat cereal, cooked like oatmeal, but there was no money to buy cereal. I did not know it at the time, but that whole wheat cereal was possibly one of the most nutritious meals that could be served.

I Timothy 6:6-8 says "But godliness with contentment is great gain. For we brought nothing into this world, and it is certain we can carry nothing out. And having food and clothing, with these we shall be content." NKJ

Butchering Time

In the winter time Pap butchered a steer or a heifer and two or three hogs. Uncle Dave Martin was the master butcher and had all the butcher tools. He came and supervised the whole operation. We cooked the meat in those big kettles over an open fire, and when the meat was ready, we would take a bite after putting some salt on it. MMMMMM! It was so delicious! The sausages were made, the slabs of dried beef were cut, and the hams were prepared for curing.

We did all of this during the time we were in Depression Years and I didn't know it! Every time we sat around the table for three meals a day, Pap would always pause for a minute or so for a silent prayer and give thanks to God.

I Thessalonians 5:18 says "In everything give thanks" and we always gave thanks for food. I Timothy 4:4-5 "For every creature of God is good, and nothing is to be refused, if it is received with thanksgiving; for it is sanctified by the word of God and prayer."

The Creek Is My Friend

The Johnny Weaver Farm was on the Cocalico Creek. For a four year old boy, it was quite a river. The creek was used for bathing in the summertime and for swimming for fun when coming from working in the field. There was a tall tree swing at the swimming hole. I learned to dive from the swing at about seven years of age. I never could figure out why the neighbor lady next to our property came at times to watch us boys swim. It created a real problem. We had to stay in the water sometimes until it got dark so that we could get out to get dressed. You see when it was only us boys swimming, we didn't bother wearing swim suits.

On one occasion it was raining all evening and we were enjoying swimming in the rain. Martin Hostetter was there with his 1930 Model A Ford so we put our clothing in his car to keep dry. When it was almost dark and the first flash of lightning hit, we all rushed into the car. Martin drove us up the steep bank and pulled under the front part of the barn. We were still scrambling for our clothing when a bolt of lightning hit a large pine tree about 50 feet away. I was frightened, near panic because I was extremely afraid of thunder and lightning. Since the rain slowed down even though the thunder and lightning was still flashing, my brothers decided to head on home. I was lagging on behind since I was the youngest making that one-fourth mile run through the meadow. Lightning flashed constantly and I was so glad to get home that night safely into the bedroom that I shared with three other brothers. After the summer rain storm we would sometimes see the beautiful rainbow appearing in the sky and Pap would tell us that it is a sign that God is remembering His promises to His children. Genesis 9:11-15

Just up the creek by the swimming hole was where James and Vera Weaver lived (also Black Bumper Mennonites.) Vera told us how inspiring the Cleona Campmeeting was and how they enjoyed those services. Another seed was planted in my heart that would cry out for reality.

The Cold Winter of 1936

Snow was on the ground much of the winter of 1936 and it was very cold. My friend, the creek, was frozen so we would go skating on the weekends. Pap was quite a skater. He said when he was young, he could skate backwards as well as forward. Well, that was a challenge to me. I would practice skating until I could skate backwards with ease. It was fun being a master on skates and pulling my younger brothers and sisters on the sled.

In February 1936 we had snow that was very deep. Some places drifted as high as the fences. The weather warmed up a bit to melt the snow on the surface. Then it turned real cold. This caused a hard crust to form on top of the snow which made it so that you could take a sled and coast a long ways. My brother, Ivan, who is five years older and I would go coasting together on the hill in the meadow. We had lots of fun coasting on the frozen crust of the snow. Ivan would lay on the sled and I would lay on top of his back since more weight made us go faster. About half way down the hill the sled broke through the snow crust and stopped instantly. But Ivan and I continued down the hill. Now it was Ivan's belly that was used for the sled.

The spring of 1936 turned warm fast. Snow melted fast causing the streams and rivers to overflow. Thick chunks of ice broke up on the Susquehanna River creating ice dams which caused the deepest flood in history until the 1972 flood when Hurricane Agnes came through.

Mam and Pap

Mam and Pap gave birth to thirteen children. Ivan's twin sister was stillborn. And my sister, Elizabeth, had scarlet fever and rheumatic heart which developed into Saint Vitas Dance. She passed away at fourteen years of age. So eleven children were raised, seven boys and four girls, Rufus, Edna, Ivan, John, Anna, myself, Esther, David, Melvin, Harvey and Ruth.

Mam was a real Proverbs 31 woman who cared for her family and was loved by everyone. Pap was a man of few words but loved by

Lizzie Weaver, my mother.

all. I had fun helping Mam to wash the clothes, putting them through the ringer. She reminded me, "Be careful that you don't get your finger caught."

I was working in the garden one day helping to pull weeds and to dig the sweet potatoes. I needed the barn fork so John threw it to me. He accidentally misjudged and the fork went deep into my foot. While I was crying for pain and was scared, Mam soaked my foot in a bucket of warm water mixed with wood ashes. She said this would draw out any poison that may have gotten in.

I was about six or seven when I accidentally cut my forefinger on top of the first joint on my left hand. The cut that went deep into the bone should have had three or four stitches. But faithful Mam bandaged my finger and it healed up nicely. It left a neat scar so that I can remember it.

I remember the beautiful old church song that Mam sang.

"I'm pressing on the upward way. New heights I'm gaining ev'ry day; Still praying as I'm onward bound, Lord, plant my feet on higher ground.

"Lord, lift me up and let me stand, By faith on Heaven's table-land, A higher plane than I have found; Lord, plant my feet on higher ground."

I know that she sang from her heart. I am thankful for that precious memory of the past.

My Mother's Hands

Being a mother of eleven children, she had her work cut out for her. I never remember my mother being unkind to me although as a boy I did not regard the spankings I received with that same kind of philosophy! However, in later years, I no longer remembered those incidences as being acts of unkindness.

I can remember my mother's hands; they were beautiful, although by today's standards they would not be regarded as such because they were callused, rugged and rough. My mother was a seamstress, and she certainly worked with her hands in making quilts, blankets and comforts for her family during the winter months. "She seeketh wool, and flax, and worketh willingly with her hands" (Proverbs 31:13).

She relaxed when visitors came, but other than that, she was always busy. She loved to serve others, especially those of her own household. "She riseth also while it is yet night, and giveth meat to her household, and a portion to her maidens" (Proverbs 31:15). This was my mother; she rose up early in the morning in order to fry the corn meal mush and scrapple, so essential to the hearty appetites of those living on a farm. After the chores were done, again we found delight in gathering around mother's table at the end of the day.

"Strength and honour are her clothing; and she shall rejoice in time to come. She openeth her mouth with wisdom; and in her tongue is the law of kindness. She looketh well to the ways of her household, and eateth not the bread of idleness.

Her children arise up, and call her blessed; her husband also, and he praiseth her" (Proverbs 31: 25-28).

The last words of my mother - a few hours before she passed on - were "My heavenly home." She has gone to be with the Lord now, and I am thankful for the fond memories of my mother. It is so important that we express our appreciation of our mothers while they are still alive.

I would like to express my honor and my appreciation to all mothers. It is a God-given virtue and a God-given responsibility.

I cannot remember ever speaking an unkind word to my mother or father. Ephesians 6:1-3 "Children, obey your parents in the Lord; for this is right. Honour your father and mother; which is the first commandment with promise: that it may be well with you, and you may live long on the earth." NKJ

Dear Lord, Creator of the heavens and the earth, we give You praise and thanks this day for Your love and care. We ask in Jesus' name that You will continue to move by Your Spirit upon us, in us, and through us for the glory of God. Thank You for my own mother, and thank You for Christian mothers everywhere. God, we ask that You will continue to move upon all our mothers. Give them strength; give them courage; give them the ability to walk with you and to serve You in all fullness. Amen.

Truly children, rise up and call your mothers blessed. God, we praise You, and we thank You for our mothers. Let Your hand be upon each of them for blessing. Let the mothers of our nations move by Your Spirit, in Jesus' name. Amen.

School

In the fall of 1932 I bravely went to the end of the lane with Edna, Ivan, John and Anna to meet the old (cracker box) Reo bus. Mr. Hipshman, the bus driver, took me in and lifted me across his lap since there was room for a little boy like me on the other side of the bus driver's seat. The first thing I did when we got to school was that I went to the teacher and told her I forgot my certificate. This certificate was the paper from our family doctor certifying that I had received the small pox vaccination.

Well, I decided to like school so it was fun and I gained many friends. My close friends were Billy Hastler and Jimmy Frey. For lunch everyday, Mam made egg sandwiches since she knew that they were nourishing for us. However, I got so tired of eating the same thing everyday. Marble playing was popular and playing for keeps was practiced by some. Ivan became a master shooter and it seemed that he had the biggest collection. I received a plaque for memorizing the times tables 1-12 in second grade.

Moving Time Again

April 1, 1936 after six short years of living on the Johnny Weaver Farm, it was sold. The farm was purchased by Martin Zimmerman. We found the Shirk Farm just 2 miles north. Pap was getting more modern because he had his 1930 Farmall 10-20 with steel wheels converted to rubber tires. This was a great day for the boys and Pap's life. Of course, he never said much but you could tell when he was pleased about something.

The worn down farm was restored in every way. By careful farming and proper fertilizing, this farm was brought to top production. It was on this farm that I learned to pray and received Jesus as my Saviour.

Instead of big Cocalico Creek, we had a small stream flowing through our farm. So under the supervision of Rufus and Ivan, we collected some stones on a farm wagon and proceeded to build a dam across this small stream. I was down in the stream stacking the stones. One of my brothers threw another stone and it caught my little finger on my right hand and broke the bone. Well, a visit to the family doctor and about 6 weeks of splints and bandages served the purpose.

Shooting Rats

Pap said when he had the Mack Truck, it seemed he always had some extra money. So he bought a Reo truck and used it for a short while for custom hauling and some farm work. It was this truck that was parked in the wagon shed when I had borrowed Ivan's 22 rifle and quietly went in front of the truck to the corn crib where the rats were eating corn. I did not like rats so I wanted to kill them.

There was a problem with the gun discharging too easily. I cocked the 22 but it fired before I was ready and the gun was pointed toward my left foot . The bullet made its way through my shoe leaving a small hole on top of my foot but a large one in the bottom of my foot. The bullet completely shattered the bone about 2 inches back of my next to the small toe. Since Pap had left for Topeka, Kansas that morning to visit his uncle Solomon Weaver, Mam had Ivan take me to the doctor. Dr. Schauntz x-rayed my injured foot and reported to me that the bone was shattered into a thousand pieces. Through his careful treatment and God's healing power, my foot healed up without any infection setting in. For about 6 weeks I was on crutches and then back to normal walking again. Thank you, Lord!

A Trip to Hershey Park

When I was eleven years of age, my sister Edna arranged for this big event of taking her younger brothers and sisters to Hershey Park. So Pap's family car was loaded up with children and a picnic lunch was prepared.

What a day! My most exciting ride was the rollercoaster with that thrilling 65 foot drop. It was a little scary at first but I decided to take the second ride.

Harvest Time

One of the exciting times as a boy was harvest time. Pap would get the McCormick wheat binder out and I would help him grease it to get it ready. When the grain was ripe enough, we would harvest the barley and wheat by using the binder to cut the grain and tie it up into sheaves. A sheaf is a bundle of grain stalks about eight to ten inches in diameter. After Pap cut the grain we would stack the sheaves together in an upright position, so that the sun and air could fully dry the grain. Within a week or two, Harvey Burkholder would come with his large Frick threshing machine and the big Ann Arbor straw bailer empowered by a huge four cylinder tractor. When the big Case tractor was up and running, it had a beautiful sound of another harvest time. The grain was put in 100 pound burlap bags and transported to the grain bins in the barn for storage.

Mam always had the biggest meals prepared for the threshing crew, and everyone ate and was filled and quickly went back to work to get all the grain before the rains came.

Pap was one of the early ones to buy a self-propelled ten foot combine which saved us so much hard work. He was then able to use this combine to harvest for the neighbors who wanted his service.

In Matthew 9:37 and 38, Jesus said "The harvest truly is plenteous, but the labourers are few; Pray ye therefore the Lord of the harvest, that He will send forth labourers into His harvest."

CHAPTER 2
HUNGRY FOR GOD

Spiritual Progress

When I was twelve years of age, Mam gave me a New Testament which was in both the German and English language. You see, our ministers were still preaching in German and reading the Scripture text in both German and English. While listening to the German and Pennsylvania Dutch dialect, I became knowledgeable of quite a bit of German. I learned much from our ministers. But the simple plan of salvation was not taught, although faith in God and an honor and respect for His word were exemplified.

I am thankful for the day I read in the Gospel Herald how that a person can pray while he or she is working. I was so happy that day. Now my prayers would not be confined to bedtime. I read all of the Christian books that I could find. My hunger for God grew and my prayer life developed. As I look back, I can remember my hunger for God in my early teens. Anna had a little plaque on her dresser. It was a prayer and I used it many times, and memorized it.

1) "Father, guide these faulting steps today, lest I fall.
   Tomorrow is far away, today is all.
   If I should keep my feet till evening time, night will bring rest. And tomorrow, I shall climb with newer zest."

2) "Oh, may I stoop to no unworthiness in pain or sorrow
   Nor bear one bitterness of yesterday to tomorrow.
   Then Father help, these searching eyes the path to see.
   Be patient with my feebleness in step to Thee. Amen."
   – Author Unknown

Salvation by Grace through Faith

When I was sixteen years old, I with some of my friends decided to join the church. We were taken through a series of Bible teaching classes on Sunday afternoon teaching the

Martindale Mennonite Church where I got saved. Groffdale Conference and Weaverland Conference still worship here.

eighteen articles of faith which were the foundation of our church doctrines. The day came for water baptism and church membership. I was looking for a spiritual experience but I was disappointed. I had a longing to be free from sin. Romans 3:23 "For all have sinned, and come short of the glory of God."

At age eighteen, Edna (my girlfriend and wife-to-be) and I went to Martindale Sunday night church service. Lester Hoover, a young ordained minister in his early 20's, preached that night. He was telling how Jesus suffered and died for my sins. I believed what he was saying and the peace of God came into my heart. To this day I thank God for the forgiveness of sins and I rejoice that my name is written in heaven! Hallelujah! What a Saviour!

John 3:16 "For God so loved the world, that He gave His only begotten Son, that whosoever believeth in Him should not perish, but have everlasting life."

SALVATION
(A copy of Luke's Salvation Tract)

How to come into a right relationship with God:

1. All Have Sinned.

All human beings are born with a sinful nature as stated in Psalm 51:5b "In sin did my mother conceive me", and Isaiah 53:6 "All we like sheep have gone astray; we have turned every one to his own way", and Romans 3:23 "For all have sinned, and come short of the glory of God."

2. Jesus Died for You!

1 Corinthians 15:3b & 4 "...Christ died for our sins according to the Scriptures; and that He was buried, and that He rose again the third day..."

Acts 3:18 "But those things, which God before had shewed by the mouth of all His prophets, that Christ should suffer, He hath so fulfilled."

John 3:16 "For God so loved the world, that He gave his only begotten Son, that whosoever believeth in Him should not perish, but have everlasting life."

1 John 1:7 "...the blood of Jesus Christ His son cleanseth us from all sin."

3. Open your heart and mind to Jesus.

Revelation 3:20 "Behold, I stand at the door and knock: if any man hear My voice, and open the door, I will come in to him and will sup with him, and he with Me."

Matthew 11:28-30 "Come unto Me all you who labor and are heavy laden, and I will give you rest. Take My yoke upon you and learn from Me, for I am gentle and lowly in heart, and you will find rest for your souls. For My yoke is easy and My burden is light." NKJ

4. Jesus said, "You must be born again" (John 3:7b). NKJ

The New Birth, as defined in John 3:3 & 5, is a spiritual birth. When we were born as babies we had a natural birth when we entered into this world. So now as you ask Jesus into your heart, you will experience a spiritual birth known as being "born again."

Romans 10:8-10 "What saith it? The Word is nigh thee even in thy mouth, and in thy heart: that is the word of faith which we preach; That if thou shall confess with thy mouth the Lord Jesus Christ, and shall believe in thine heart that God hath raised Him from the dead, thou shall be saved. For with the heart man believeth unto righteousness; and with the mouth confession is made unto salvation."

Luke 24:47 "And that repentance and remission of sins should be preached in His name among all nations, beginning at Jerusalem."

5. Pray to Accept Christ as Personal Savior.

Pray this prayer with an open mind and heart: "Dear Lord Jesus, Son of the Living God, I'm sorry for all my sins." (Take time to mention the most prominent sins by name as they come to your mind.) "Lord Jesus, I know that you died for me to take away my sins. I confess with my mouth the Lord Jesus, and I believe in my heart that God has raised Him (Jesus) from the dead so I can be saved. Come into my heart and save me now. By your help I will turn from my wrong ways, and I want to serve you all the days of my life.

Thank you, Lord, for hearing my prayer. Amen."

Now thank the Lord for receiving you, and thank Him for writing your name in the Lamb's book of life. (Luke 10:20).

6. Now tell someone.

Tell someone what you've done, that you've accepted Jesus into your life and that you are now a new Christian. Jesus said, "Go, tell what great things God has done for you."

7. Start reading your Bible on a daily basis.

Develop a daily reading of the Bible, starting in the Gospel of Matthew. Each morning get down on your knees and thank God for rest, thank Him for keeping you, and ask the Lord to guide you and to keep you though the day. At night, thank God again for His goodness to you and develop a prayer life with Jesus as you go through the day.

8. Find a Bible believing Church.

Find a good Bible believing, Bible preaching church that

believes in the power of God and the Holy Spirit.

Pressing into God

When I was a teenager I was practicing weight pressing on a platform scale. I made a harness and put it over my shoulder and connected it to a bar held by my hand and placed it on the front of my legs. The bar was connected to the bottom of the platform scale. So with my knees slightly bent, I pulled with my hands and arms at the same time pulling with my shoulders in a standing position. By doing a lot of practice I was able to press the scale 720 pounds subtracting my body weight of 120 pounds. I conquered pressing 600 pounds at the age of fourteen.

One day our neighbor came to see us. I showed him how I could pull or press 600 pounds. He was a big strong man so he tried, but was embarrassed because he could barely do half the weight that I did. The secret was knowing how and to keep practicing at it.

Jesus said in Luke 16:16 "...the kingdom of God is preached, and every man presseth into it." It's like riding my bicycle. It's fun to coast but you can't depend on coasting. You must press the peddles if you want to get somewhere. So in our spiritual progress it is important to keep pressing into God and His word. It's all right to coast a short while on God's blessings and good feelings, but we can't depend on coasting on feelings. We must press into God's word and prayer and service.

Faith, fact and feeling sat upon a wall.
And feeling had an awful fall
And pulled down faith.
But fact remained,
And fact pulled up faith
And faith pulled up feeling too.
    – Author Unknown

You see the fact in this poem is the word of God. Humpty Dumpty fell off the wall but God's word will never fall. I do not say that feeling is not important, but you can't build upon it. You cannot build a house in the clouds, because it does not have a foundation and you can't build on feeling because feeling does not have a foundation. But thank God we can build on the word of God (The Bible). Matthew 24:35 "Heaven and earth shall pass away, but My words shall not pass away." Ephesians 2:20 "And are built upon the foundation of apostles and prophets, Jesus Christ Himself being the chief cornerstone."

My commitment is to read God's word every day and to have daily prayer and devotion. At the time of this writing I'm into my 32nd time to read the Bible through in a year's time. I use a marker for both the Old and New Testament. I take the number of pages in the Old Testament and divide it into twelve. In my Bible, it comes to 78 pages per month. In my New Testament it is 24 pages per month.

A recent picture of a 1950 8N Ford tractor.

The Corn Field Preacher

Pap was introduced to the new 1940 Farmall H, a new and modern tractor model. Well, you can guess. He made the deal. Now that my bigger brothers were all working away from home, I, then at the age of fourteen, became the number one farmer for Pap and I loved it. That tractor was my friend. However, after the novelty of the new tractor had warn off, the Farmall H became my pulpit working alone in the corn field. I would envision a large group of people before me (and my voice being drowned out by the sound of the working tractor), I would preach to these "people." I wish I could remember what I preached. As I look back on this I realized it was God's calling on my life for the ministry of the word. This was all kept secret.

Jesus Saves

When I finished sowing a large field of wheat one day, I had some grain left in the grain drill. So I decided to write in large letters across the field "Jesus Saves" in order to be a witness to the airplane pilots. Our farm was located on the air route from Reading to Lancaster.

CHAPTER 3
IN LOVE

*I am at the left of the center row with my
brothers and sisters in 1940.*

My Sister Edna's Wedding

Wedding bells brought excitement to our house on October
24, 1940. My sister, Edna, became married to Frank Weaver.
We had to do a lot of work around the farm to get ready for
the all day wedding at the farm house. Bishop Joe Hostetter
preached his sermon before performing the ceremony. After
the ceremony, the big wedding dinner was served in shifts to
feed the guests.

The afternoon session was a time of singing church songs
and hymns which was led by Uncle Amos who had the ability
to lead and he loved group singing. I took my place at the
end of the middle row of chairs and then my sister, Anna,
came with Frank's two sisters, Anna Mary and Edna.

Well, Anna kindly shoved this pretty little fourteen year old
Edna ahead of her into the chair right next to me. She had

the prettiest sparkling blue eyes and lovely groomed black hair. Well, Edna was so shy and embarrassed that she at first refused to hold the song book which we were sharing. But she decided to hold the book since she was more embarrassed not to.

As far as I was concerned, things were working out just fine. I was in love with this beauty and I was so excited that day. I think this was the greatest day of my life so far. One of the songs that Uncle Amos led was "Does Jesus Care?" which goes like this in the chorus "Oh yes, He cares. I know He cares." This seemed to be a spiritual experience as well as an emotional experience of love for my new teen sweetheart. I guess I was walking on air the rest of the day.

That afternoon, I changed into my work clothes early to do the evening chores. So I was in the family picture with my work clothes. It was a good thing that I did the chores early so that I was able to be back in the house in time to see Edna leave with her sister, Esther, and husband, Sam. When Edna was going down the open stairway, I threw some confetti on her. She responded with that sweet smile and the bells were beginning to ring in my heart.

That night I knelt at my bedside and prayed "Oh God! Please bless my precious Edna. Protect her, watch over her and keep her. In Jesus' name. Amen."

Speechless

Edna got sick and was taken to Lancaster Hospital for an appendicitis operation. I was out in the field one day and I went in the midst of the tall corn and knelt down on the ground and asked God to heal Edna. Thank God, her recovery was speedy!

Just about a week after she came home from the hospital, my cousin, Edwin Martin, drove my friend, Paul Good, and me in Uncle Amos's car to the Henry Weaver farm. We found Edna sitting in her father's car near the road by the barn. Edwin drove right next to Edna but I became speechless. I could not say a word. I guess I just looked at this beautiful girl and smiled. My cousin soon drove off since I wasn't going to talk. They sure made fun of me since I didn't speak to her. Here I was fifteen years old and in love with a beautiful young farm girl named Edna Mae Weaver.

Later on I learned from Edna, my teen sweetheart, that she had spent the summer with her Aunt Stella who lived across the Cocalico Creek at the same time my family lived on the Johnny Weaver Farm. So it was possible that I could have met her at the age of nine or ten and didn't know then that she was going to be my wife.

Dilemma Turned into Blessing

Now, how can I get to see my new sweetheart? She was so precious. I was only fifteen years old and was not allowed to date officially until I reached seventeen and a half. Thursday night was the shopping time in Ephrata. Maybe perchance I

Edna at age 15 on the left with her sisters,
Esther and Anna Mary.

could see her there and just get one more of her beautiful heart warming smiles.

On January 4, 1941, my sister Anna invited a group of girlfriends for a Sunday dinner. The invitation included Anna Mary and Edna. That Saturday night a light snow had fallen and it was a most beautiful sunny winter day. My sweetheart was the focal point of my life even though my conversation with Edna was very little that day. It was a day I have never forgotten, Edna with her orange dress and the sun shining in my heart.

Springtime came and Frank and Edna took to housekeeping in the back part of Edna's parents' house. Now there was hope of seeing my teenage sweetheart. My parents visited Edna and Frank about twice a month on a Tuesday night. Only a few words were usually shared. Sometime in the spring or summer of 1941 my sister Edna and Frank had us go to her house for Sunday dinner. I was disappointed because Edna was not at home since she was at Aunt Lydia's house helping her with the Sunday dinner which was prepared for her guests. By 2:30 that afternoon she finished up. So after dinner, Clarence, her brother, invited me to go with him to pick her up. I took the freedom to sit next to Edna on our way back. As I looked at her and was by now talking to her freely, her beauty overwhelmed me. She had those beautiful eye brows and beautiful blue eyes and had neatly groomed black hair puffed up enough to make some waves in her hair that was beautifully combed to cover the top of her ears. Clarence seemed to be very happy to see his sister in love with me. Well, the dilemma seemed to be turning into blessings!

A Walk in the Meadow

"Pap, may I have the car to visit Paul Good?" Now Paul was my best friend. This was granted with a nod of the head and "Uh, Huh." Now I had heard somehow that Edna was over at her sister, Esther and Sam's house. So I quickly drove over to Paul's folks and to my great delight no one was at home. So

Pap's 1938 model Packard found its way even more quickly to my sweetheart's sister's home where we spent the afternoon together.

On another Sunday afternoon, Edna and I drove over to the old swimming hole and walked through the two meadows near the Cocalico Creek. We then crossed over the swinging walkway bridge over the Cocalico Creek toward the north side pasture. We were holding hands, walking and talking and I said to her "I wonder what the next ten years will have for us." My faith in God was increasing. The time spent with her was so precious.

Again as I knelt at my bedside that night after the lights were out, I silently but earnestly prayed "Lord, please bless and protect Edna. Be good to her in every way. She is so sweet and I love her so much. Lord, if it is your will for Edna to be my life companion, work out all the details. Amen." I guess most of my prayers were for my sweetheart and for myself so I could be a proper companion for Edna. If God chose to take us through life in marriage, my desire also was to be lovers all the days of our lives. Proverbs 18:22 "Whoso finds a wife findeth a good thing, and obtaineth favour of the Lord."

Young man and young woman, seek God with all of your heart for God's blessing and God's direction for your life companionship. It is a great blessing to be committed to your spouse and your spouse committed to you. Nothing shall separate us from the love of Christ and from each other.

The 1939 Packard

In May of 1943, the war was getting more intense. I was seventeen years old and young men my age were being drafted into the military. Parents who lost their sons and daughters in the war went through a lot of heartaches. My church took a peace stand since we literally lived by what the Sermon on the Mount had taught us. Matthew 5:39 says "But I say unto you, that ye resist not evil: but whosoever shall smite thee on

Edna by the 1939 Packard.

thy right cheek, turn to him the other also" and Matthew 5:44 says "But I say unto you, love your enemies, bless them that curse you, do good to them that hate you, and pray for them which despitefully use you, and persecute you." So when I registered at the age of eighteen, I applied for the conscientious objector (C.O.) which exempted me from all military activities. Also since I was Pap's main farmer, I was granted a 4E classification, a deferred farmer status.

It was in those days that I said to my Dad, "Pap, will you go with me to buy a car?" I was able to purchase a 1939 Packard for $600. By now I was given the permission to date even though it was about three months before the official dating age. My parents knew I was in love with Edna, so by all appearance I had their approval. In 1950 I sold the Packard for $250. Years later, I saw some antique Packards in a museum in Victoria, British Columbia. There was one similar to mine restored. That 1939 Packard fully restored today would be worth $50,000 at the time of this writing. I guess I should have kept it. Now the beautiful blue Packard had even the bumpers and grill painted black because this was the church rule.

Juniata County

There was a funeral of one of our relatives in Juniata County. I offered to drive my Packard to take Pap and his brother, Uncle Bishop Joe Weaver, to the funeral. On the way, one of my tires went flat and was beyond repair. Now that I was using the spare tire, we needed to shop for a used tire quickly to replace the spare tire. So we stopped at two or three places hoping to find a used tire. However, there were no tires available because it was wartime and all tires had to be sent to the military. So I said "I guess we will have to trust the Lord." Uncle Joe confirmed the statement and agreed that we should do more of that. We did make it the rest of the way with no more flat tires! God is good!

CHAPTER 4
COURTSHIP

The Henry Weaver House built in 1761.

Big Four

The Packard served me well all through courtship and early marriage. Because we were in war time and pleasure driving was prohibited, I would go to Edna's house first for a date on Saturday night before going over to my sister, Edna, and Frank's for the night and then on to Weaverland Church on Sunday. So I reasoned that this would make my Sunday driving legal.

Courtship was a privilege. Six of us young people took a trip to Endless Caverns and Natural Bridge in Virginia. We carried extra gas in the trunk of the car. Gas could only be purchased with gas stamps in addition to money. I could hardly wait for the next date. It was probably around our eighteenth birthday. Edna is only five weeks younger than I am. One night I told Edna,"I want you to be my wife" and she beautifully responded,"I want you to be my husband." Later on that year I asked Pap if he would sign for my marriage license. He declined with a remark that I was too young. Well, that put things on hold for a while.

By spring of 1945 Pap rented the Eberly Farm which was about a mile and a half away. Since the house on this farm was empty, I came up with an idea that this would be a good time to ask Pap again. So I took the courage and asked Pap again if I could get married and his response with a smile was "Will we need to plant the garden?" This was his way of making a statement of approval!

Edna, age 16.

Our church had Saturday night singings. This was announced by word of mouth several weeks in advance. The first part of the evening was spent by singing as a group. Then later on in the evening they would start the "Big Four." This was similar to a square dance with the music of a harmonica, or an accordion and, in a few instances, an acoustic guitar. Edna loved the "Big Four" and somehow I thought this was not right. Edna usually helped to get it started. As soon as the boys started to join in she would check out. I guess she did this so I wouldn't get jealous.

In summer and fall some of the young people would announce a "crowd" that was arranged by their parents who would put on a meal for all the young people. This could be from 100 to 200 young people. This was a great time of fellowship and fun. The fellows would ask the girls for dates and would take them home in their cars. Many times they would ask to take them out on a date at the next Saturday night's singing. At times this would develop into going steady and then later into marriage.

Some of the Sunday nights when they did not have a crowd, we would go to Edna's church at Weaverland or Martindale. During fall or spring we visited the United Zion Revival

Meetings. This was a small plain denomination that believed in holiness and it was acceptable to demonstrate joy right in church. We went for the entertainment to see who would get happy or have a shouting spell. Well, these people were for real and I believe a bit of their glory had an influence on my life. You see if you get a taste of the fire of God you will never be satisfied with just formality.

CHAPTER 5
OUR WEDDING

July 14, 1945

Now it had gotten very busy at Edna's house. The quilts for the bride's wedding gifts were already started and needed to be finished. Everything around the farm needed to be put away in proper order. The wedding day was set for Saturday July the 14th, 1945, right in the middle of harvest time. Bishop

Our wedding picture.

A recent picture of Edna's sisters quilting.

Paul Graybil performed the ceremony. We were both nineteen and a half years old. Edna was so beautiful in her light blue wedding dress. It was years later that white dresses and church weddings became common.

Edna was a member of Lancaster Conference Mennonite Church and I was a member of the Weaverland Conference better known to many as the "Black Bumpers." Again I learned the wisdom of Mam for she encouraged me to join Edna's church. So I became a member of Edna's church before we were married. This is a very important part of a successful marriage and that is to become members of the same local church.

My sister, Esther, was Edna's maid of honor and her boyfriend, Willis Martin, was my best man at our wedding. The dinner that my mother-in-law prepared was so delicious and the wedding guests ate in shifts. Because it was such a busy time of the year, Aunt Alta remarked to Edna in a joke, "Don't ever get married again in July!" The old Henry Weaver Homestead had many weddings. The house was built in 1761 and the old barn was built in 1764.

Our Honeymoon

We spent our first night at Edna's home in the guest room. I just couldn't fall asleep. I needed to sleep where it was cooler, so I finally laid on the bedroom floor and got some sleep that night. This became a common practice many times. Many times I would wake up on the floor but not because she pushed me out of bed. It would seem that if I would get a bit warm, I would be looking for a cooler place even in my sleep.

On the second night, we went to the farm house near Denver, Pennsylvania. Honeymoons were not a common practice in those days. Some of the couples took "wedding trips" together. On Sunday, July 15, 1945, the day after our wedding, it started to rain and it rained everyday for 40 days. Much of the harvest in the field spoiled. On Monday, Anna Mary and Ivan took us to Philadelphia where we had our first ride on the subway train, had lunch out and did some shopping. The old farm house was quiet and a bit lonely for Edna especially if she was at home alone. So we enjoyed the forty days of rain together. I guess you can call this our honeymoon.

In September, John Martin and Ella Zimmerman got married and Edna and I went with them on a wedding trip to Niagara Falls, NY for two days. We stopped at a restaurant for lunch and a man turned his chair to watch us. When we went to pay the bill, we were told that it was already paid for. We figured he saw a good show, these very plain dressed young people. Niagara Falls was beautiful and we took a ride on the "Maid of the Mist" Boat that took us real close to the bottom of the Falls. We all put rain coats and hats on to keep from getting wet. Our wedding trip to Niagara Falls was fun and very enjoyable as we traveled in John Martin's 1941 Ford.

The Eberly Farm near Denver, Pennsylvania

Edna and I were happily married. We did not have a telephone. Also we did not have electric hook up with the power line. We had a Delco 32 volt electric system that gave us lights. The generator on the tower with a wind propeller

The Eberly Farm where we set up housekeeping.

was out of commission. Our refrigerator was an old fashioned ice box. We had to put a 30 pound block of ice in it about twice a week to keep the refrigerator cool at all times.

We worked together in the garden and yard. Edna is a good house keeper. She does not like to leave a stack of dirty dishes around. She cleans them up after every meal. The bed is properly made first thing each morning. Our 1939 Packard still had the black bumper and grill even though I had joined Edna's church six month earlier. So one day out under the big maple tree, Edna and I started to take the paint off the bumpers. But when we started taking it off the grill, it was more difficult and we worked long and hard. We finally did accomplish the task. We were now members of the Lancaster Conference and the bumpers were not required to be black.

Pap had some sheep in our farm and Mam made a comfort from the sheep wool. I had a beautiful flock of Rhode Island red chickens. They produced large brown eggs. The tobacco crop on the Eberly farm was my project so I received half of the selling price and Henry Eberly received the other half.

Henry was Mam's cousin. One of the things we were taught as Mennonites was to be good stewards of our money. Edna took a job in Moyer's Factory in Ephrata, so she rode with my second cousin to the factory.

Now to be good stewards, it was important to turn off any electric light in any room that was not in use. So Edna's factory driver kept the car lights off in the dark for the purpose of saving electricity. The humor of this was that she did not realize that her source of lighting the car lights was free of charge whether she used them or not.

Hunting season came and 1945 had lots of pheasants on our farm. I was using Pap's Nickerbocker twelve gauge double barrel shot gun. Somehow that day I was able to hit the flying pheasants. I brought twelve birds in that day. Well, a bit of conviction came when Edna questioned this "Isn't the limit two per day?" Well, I tried to make some kind of excuse. I said, "You see, it is on our own farm." (See Restitution.)

Winter time came and we had heavy snow. Our lane and road was blown shut with snow. Now through my encouragement, Pap had a snow plow built on the Farmall H tractor. The new snow plow didn't work properly because it needed a lift. So I took the tractor to the welding shop to have the hydraulic lift fastened to the snow plow. It was a long day of work and I didn't get home until several hours after dark. Well, I couldn't call home to tell Edna that I was running late because we didn't have a telephone and I couldn't drive home by car because the roads were closed due to the snowdrifts. I couldn't go with the snow plow because it didn't work. My precious wife was left alone and she was fearful after dark. When she saw me plowing my way home, she decided to go to bed and not talk to me. This was our first confrontation in our marriage because I had mistreated her by coming home late. Well, instead of going out and doing the chores I stayed with her and comforted her and she forgave me for coming home late.

"Edna, I Love You"

I purpose to say to Edna every day, "Edna, I love you," because God has given me a precious jewel.

Proverbs 18:21 "The tongue can kill or nourish life." NLT

Proverbs: 18:22 "The man who finds a wife finds a treasure and receives favor from the Lord." NLT

Psalms 34:1 "I will bless the Lord at all times; His praise shall continually be in my mouth."

From these verses we see it is important to express praise and love to our God and to our spouses.

Family Started

Edna was expecting our first child, so we had a friendly argument. She said "I want a girl" and I said "I want a boy." She insisted I wanted a girl; and I with more emphasis said, by mistake, "I want a girl" with laughter. Edna won the argument.

September 9, 1946 Irene was born.

April 26, 1948 Melvin was born.

December 1, 1949 Earl was born.

May 29, 1952 Martha was born.

July 26, 1954 Luke was born.

"Daddy, Why Do You Spank Me?"

It was our practice to tuck our little ones in bed and pray for them and kiss them good night. On one occasion when Earl was about two and a half years old, I tucked him into bed and gave him two or three kisses on his cheek and forehead as I would usually do every night. That night, he looked up at me and said, "Daddy, why do you kiss me so often?" Because I love you, Earl." "Daddy, why do you spank me?" "Because I love you, Earl. You see our Heavenly Father loves Daddy and sometimes my Father in Heaven needs to spank Daddy also because He loves me." Read Hebrews 12:5-11.

Roses

Our life has been like roses, lots of blessings and love. But roses also have thorns and they can hurt you if you don't handle them carefully.

When I was fifteen years old and I met Edna unexpectedly, I was speechless. Well, in our marriage, communication has been a problem. So Edna and I went to a Christian Counselor. As the three of us met together, it seemed that a miracle happened and God helped us. Now God is helping us to handle the roses properly.

For a good marriage, keep communication open between each other.

CHAPTER 6
FROM SWITZERLAND

Henry and Martha Weaver and their 10 children.

Henry and Martha Weaver

Our stay at the Eberly Farm was short - from July 14, 1945 to March 1946. On April 1, 1946 we moved to the back part of the Henry Weaver Farm house in Weaverland and I became Henry's farmer for three years. I enjoyed my in-laws, Henry and Martha Weaver. I never had any unkind words from my mother-in-law. She was a precious woman. She took her trip to heaven in May of 1987. About a year before she died, I asked her one day to tell me about the time she saw heaven. It was at the birth of one of her children that she nearly died or had an out-of-body experience. Mom saw herself leaving her body and being taken up. She had a glimpse of the city of light. "Mom, please tell us what you saw." "Oh, it was so beautiful. I don't have words to tell you" was her reply. In her last years as she had a number of hospital experiences and during the last ten months of her life, she lived at the Fairmont

Home. All of the nurses and workers loved her. Henry and Martha Weaver had thirteen children. Three died as infants. Martha was a Proverbs 31 woman.

Henry was such a fine lovely man loved by everyone. He went on to be with the Lord in 1965 after three weeks of suffering from a stroke. At Henry's viewing, there were 300 people who came to the house and on the day of his funeral, the Weaverland Church was filled with people standing by the sidewalls. People sure loved Henry. The attendance at the funeral was 1,000.

Clarence to California

After corn planting, I took Edna's brother, Clarence, and Uncle Joe Weaver in the Packard to California. Clarence was in the Army in the paratrooper division and was transferred from Kentucky to California. Uncle Joe had a son, Aaron, in Hollywood, California. So we headed west and as a young man I desired to see the west, because Pap being a country pal, traveled in his motorcycle all through the north out to Washington and California before he was married. It took us 72 hours to get to California. Clarence and I took turns driving. We spent three days in California and visited Yosemite National Park and drove the 1939 Packard under the large redwood tree which was about eighteen feet in diameter. It took Uncle Joe and me five days to return home. Thanks to God and the Packard.

*The drive through a tree in Yosemite National Park with
Clarence, Uncle Joe and cousin Aaron*

Our Ancestors from Switzerland

Johann Anton Weaver came from Switzerland in 1711. They had five children, four boys and a girl. Their son, Georg, was my family tree and one of their other sons, Heinrich (Henry), was Edna's family tree. So in recent years while studying this family tree, I discovered that Edna and I are seventh cousins. It was our same Grandpa generations ago that came from Switzerland.

The Mennonites were persecuted because they were Anabaptists. The laws of the land required every baby to be baptized in the state church which was the Reformed Church. In the 1620's, Georg Blourock, Philix Manz and Conrad Grebel became believers in the Lord. They were baptized as believers and many of the Swiss followed. Some were put in prison while others were drowned in the Zurich River. About nine generations ago, our Great Grandfather, Georg Weber, who lived in a town called Kyburg near Winterthur, was imprisoned with Jacob Ammann who later founded the Amish Church. Our Great Grandfather was martyred in 1639 for being baptized as a believer. Because of persecution, our relatives came to America to raise their families with religious freedom. They suffered many hardships, but their faith in the Lord brought them through.

Inside the prison cell in Kyburg, Switzerland

In Zermatt, Switzerland

In 1991, Edna and I were privileged to visit Switzerland. It was a great blessing to us to visit the land of our forefathers. The large cathedral, The Gros Munster, was already built when our ancestors were living there. We saw the Wassercarich where they had devices used for persecution.

We visited a cave in Canton Zurich. The cave was called the Anabaptist Cave. This was a place of hiding for the Anabaptists. Since our family was from that area, we believe that our relatives had hidden in this cave. Visiting here was a solemn moment for us, knowing that they were praying for their offspring.

The Anabaptist's cave where they hid away.

We also were moved when we visited the Kyburg Castle (near Winterthur) the home area of Georg Weber. Edna and I were in the two prison cells, and also in the torture room where our Grandfather was martyred in 1639. He was killed for believing in and being baptized as an adult.

Here I am nine generations later and have taught the message of believers baptism to thousands of people and have directed many believers baptism services.

Great Grandpa Henry Weaver

Young Henry decided to go to Ontario, Canada to settle down in this new frontier land and work on a farm. I remember Edna's grandfather, Frank Weaver, and my father-in-law Henry telling the story. One day Henry went to help a neighbor farmer put some hay into the barn after it was cut and dried. They would put the hay in piles before loading them onto the wagon. As they drove their horses pulling the hay wagon from pile to pile, one of the farmers would take a long handled hay fork and lift the hay pile onto the wagon. The other helper would carefully load the hay folding it over in layers so that all of the hay would stay together on the wagon while it was being transported over the rough field on the way to the barn.

By mid-afternoon the farmer's daughter came out with a small pail of drinking water for her daddy and his helper, Henry. As she started back to the house up at the corner of the field next to the woods, she decided to lay down and rest on one of the soft hay piles. It was so soft and smelled so good. As she rested a few minutes, she fell asleep. While stacking the hay, Henry and the farmer saw a wolf coming out of the forest and doing something at one of the hay piles. After awhile they came to the hay pile where they had seen the wolf and they found the farmer's daughter sleeping on one of the piles. They noticed that she was covered with hay. It appeared that the wolf had spotted her sleeping and was making plans to come back to capture her possibly after dark. That's why the wolf covered her. So they woke the girl up and took her into the house away from the danger of the wolf. Afterwards, Henry and the farmer went back to work. When it got dark, they went to the cabin and had a fine farmer's meal. After supper, the farmer advised Henry to stay over night. He said it could be very dangerous at night because of the wolves.

Henry, being very brave, said that he was not afraid and believed that he could get home safely. After walking along the road for awhile, he decided to cut across the woods for a shortcut. Soon he saw and heard in the dark two wolves following him. He got himself a good stick and started running, and at the end of the lane he climbed up into a tree to rest. By then, there were three wolves howling around the tree. As he rested, he heard more wolves howling all over the forest. Well, one thing for sure, he couldn't spend the night in the tree. So he took his stick and jumped out of the tree, fought the wolves away with his stick and ran as hard as he could for the cabin. The door opened in and he fell on the floor. The door closed since it was built to latch by itself. After he had rested for awhile, he looked out of the window. The moon had gotten brighter and by now he could see many wolves howling around the tree where they could smell his scent.

Henry didn't like the cold winter and the late spring. So in the first week of May as he was watering the horses, he took them to the stream nearby. The ice was still strong enough to carry the weight of the horses. So Henry said to himself, "If the heavy horses do not break through the ice in the first week of May, I will return to Weaverland and settle down there." Sure enough, the heavy team of horses did not break the ice during that first week of May. So Henry left Ontario to return to Weaverland and settle down, which was around 1848.

God did all this to put my marriage together. He arranged for Edna and me to meet at the right time. God has given us a goodly heritage. Psalm 16:6 says "The lines are fallen unto me in pleasant places; yea, I have a goodly heritage."

CHAPTER 7
HEALING BY GOD'S WORD

The Reality of Healing

In 1949, T. L. Osborne and Gorden Lindsey came with a large tent to Reading, Pennsylvania where they held their Osborne-Lindsey Healing Campaign. We went several nights and saw the sick being healed and many people getting saved. This brought on a great impact in my life. Revival fires were burning.

Gerald Derstine got saved in this revival and was healed of chronic stammering. I was freely talking to others about Jesus and how Jesus heals the sick. My relatives became greatly concerned about me and gave some words of caution. My cousin gave me a book that was teaching against divine healing. Since it was so well written, I decided that this healing movement was of the devil. I even taught this publicly in the Sunday School Class in the Denver Mennonite Church.

Our children in 1955.

While I took a stand against healing during this time, Edna and I got more and more traditional. We got plainer and plainer, believing this would please God. I bought a plainer suit, a frock tail coat, the kind the bishops wore during that time. I parted my hair in the middle and pressed it down real flat so as not to have any appearance of worldliness. This was all done trusting that we would be more pleasing to God. I was so strict that no amount of money could have convinced me to wear a neck tie. I encouraged Edna to dress plainer and plainer. The girls did not have any lace on their dresses. We were sold out to the traditional plain dress. I started to teach that men should not shave but grow beards for the Lord's sake. Edna was not too excited about this and I respected her but with some hesitation. After all of this, the hunger in our hearts was yet not satisfied. We were still asking ourselves, "What is the answer that would bring us spiritual fulfillment?"

Then James Bucher came to the Hinkeltown Mennonite Church for a week of revival meetings. Now, Brother Bucher was greatly respected by those of us who were promoting the plain dress. On Sunday, he announced a healing service for Monday night. The church was packed on Monday night. I was part of the pre-service prayer meeting. I spoke a prayer request. "I request that God will have His way tonight because there will be some people in the meeting that are following those fanatical healing campaigns." Dear Brother Bucher commented in his deep but kind voice, "Just because there is some fanaticism around, it should not keep us from preaching the truth." I felt like falling through a crack in the floor. So I listened to an outstanding sermon on divine healing that night. Brother Bucher preached with freedom and with power and authority. He was preaching God's word from Exodus 15:26 "I am the Lord that healeth thee," Isaiah 53:5 "But He was wounded for our transgressions, He was bruised for our iniquities: the chastisement of our peace was upon Him; and with His stripes we are healed," and Matthew 8:17 "He Himself took our infirmities and bore our sicknesses." NKJ

I was hearing the same message that T. L. Osborne had preached four years earlier. I said to myself, "What shall I do? I respect this man of God." So my lips became silent on the subject of divine healing and I started studying the Bible on this subject more earnestly. Some time afterwards, I bought a book at a rummage sale for ten cents. It was T. L. Osborne's *Healing the Sick and Casting Out the Devil*. As I was reading this book it was basically the same message that James Bucher preached at the revival meetings. I was becoming a believer again in God's healing power for today. I then disposed of T. L. Osborne's book because I wanted to make sure that I based my teaching of divine healing solely on the Word of God and not on man's doctrines.

God Heals Our Children

With the healing message revived in my heart, Edna and I started praying for our children when they were sick. Martha was barely two years old when she was sick with a fever. By now the miracle drugs were already in use such as sulfa and penicillin. Martha's temperature was a bit over 103. Edna and I laid hands on her and asked Jesus to heal her. In fifteen minutes according to my watch, I took her temperature again and it had come down to 101. Now that was faster then what the miracle drug could do. Praise God for His healing power. Next time when our children got sick, we called the same Doctor.

Irene, who was about seven years old at the time, had nearly 30 warts on her hands. The children at school did not like to hold her hands on the playground because of the warts. Doctors had a way of burning them out. We told Irene that Jesus could heal her if she asked us to pray for her or we could take her to the doctor if she preferred. Sometime later Irene asked us to pray for the healing of her warts so Edna and I led a simple prayer by placing our hands upon her and asked Jesus to heal her of those warts. We all forgot about the warts until about two weeks later at the dinner table when I remembered and said, "Oh, Irene, how are your hands?" And we all looked and praise God for the warts were all gone.

On another occasion Marty injured her foot. For about three or four days she could not put any weight upon it. It had swollen a lot and turned dark blue and green. At that time we were trusting God completely and believing it was wrong for us to go to doctors. One night this injured foot was hurting her so bad that she could not sleep. However, the next morning while Edna and I were up early praying in the living room, Marty ran across the living room and said "Daddy, I'm healed!" She said that I had gone into her bedroom last night and prayed for her. I must have been more asleep than awake because I didn't remember going into her room to pray for her. Well, whatever the problem was with her foot, we knew that the healing was a miracle from God and we were so thankful for His healing power.

When we lived on 40th Street, Mel and Earl got to quarreling about something. Then Earl got on his bicycle to get away from Mel. It started raining, so he quickly turned back to get out of the rain. However, something happened to his front wheel causing it to lock which made the bike tip over. Earl was then thrown onto the road right in front of a moving car. The driver of the car was scared but was able to avoid hitting him. Earl's arm was injured and it appeared to be fractured. When he got home, he went straight to his bedroom and cried because he was hurting from the severe pain.

I asked him if he would have been ready if his life was taken. He answered, "No." So I led Earl to Jesus. He was so happy. Then I handed his own Bible to him and asked him to open it to see what promise the Lord would give him. He reached up and took the Bible by the hand that had been badly injured just minutes before. Earl was instantly healed by the power of God!

CHAPTER 8 - REVIVAL

Revival Fires in Lancaster

In 1951, George and Lawrence Brunk came to Lancaster with their large tent and held revival meetings at the East Chestnut Street Mennonite Church and the Lord sent revival. People were getting saved and others were committing their lives to the Lord. It was in this tent meeting revival that Mam and Pap went to the prayer tent for the assurance of salvation and God did a precious work in their hearts.

The revival fires kept burning so they moved the tent to the old airport grounds. The revival continued every night for seven weeks. Crowds were estimated to be up to 15,000 people on a Sunday afternoon.

Edna and I were in nearly all of those meetings. We were hungry for God and were rejoicing in the spirit of revival. In 1954 Edna and I responded to a missionary call at a missionary conference in Lancaster. Pastor Raymond Charles prayed over us so beautifully and asked God to give us direction in His service.

Children

Irene and Melvin were both precious children. By now I had decided that I was going to teach my children not to smoke or use tobacco. About three months later one Sunday morning at Weaverland Church, God spoke to my heart that I should give up tobacco farming. The Lord said "Why do you raise it for others if you don't want your own family to use it?" I said "Yes, Lord, this is my last year of farming tobacco." Because we gave up tobacco farming, we moved from Weaverland to the farm north of Ephrata where Pap and Mam lived. Then on December 1, 1949, Earl was born. He was a big ten pound baby.

Fox Street Mission

Early in 1955, we took a trip to New York to see Bishop Amos Horst sail for Europe on a ministry trip. While we were there, we visited the Mennonite Mission on 1128 Fox Street, in the Bronx, New York City with Pastor and Mrs. Aquila Rheal. They invited us to come and work with them. So we started going to Fox Street Mennonite Mission every two weeks. On each of these Sundays, we would get up early to milk the cows and do all of the other chores before driving 160 miles to the Bronx, in time for Sunday School. On several of these occasions we would arrive there before they unlocked the doors.

To get to church on time is very simple. You just get started on time.

On one of these trips, I took a group of young people along. One of the girls' Dad let us use his station wagon. We had a fun time together. On the way home on this particular Sunday afternoon, the boy friend of this girl wanted to drive. His request was granted reluctantly on my part. Traveling in New Jersey on U.S. Route 1, our young driver made a mistake and crashed into another car. One of the girls had a whiplash that showed up later on. A wrecker towed the car off the highway. I called a friend to come and pick us up. After waiting three hours in a restaurant, our friend arrived to carry us home in his station wagon.

Back in those years I felt it was wrong in all cases to spend any money on Sundays unless it was absolutely necessary. So I had this group of teens for three long hours sipping water. My, my, I was strict.

"I'll Go Where You Want Me To Go"
By Edna Weaver

The song I used to sing "I'll go where You want me to go, over the mountain, over the plain, over the sea" was my song until one day the Lord put me to the test. Then the Lord

Our 5 children in the late 1950's.

spoke to us about moving to New York City after going there helping with the mission. But I said leaving the farm with five little children sure did not look like wisdom to me and people were advising against it. Then the Lord reminded me that I said "I'll go where He wants me to go and promised never to say 'no' when I am asked to do something." Then the Lord said "If it is your five children standing in your way, I can take two of them away. Then you have only three." I visualized myself being at their funeral. From then on we started getting ready for the mission in New York City in the Bronx no matter what anyone said. We started buying things like games, etc. since our children could not go out to play like they were used to playing on the farm. I said "If God sends us, He will equip us for He is able to do exceedingly abundantly above what we are able to ask or think."

After we became willing to go, that door closed for us and another door opened for us to go to Harrisburg, Pennsylvania to help with the mission there. This experience helped us to know that God looks inside our hearts and sees spiritual pride in us. He had to remove this pride in us to make us better able to help others. So He fixed a fix for us! Afterwards whenever I would hear a church full of people singing "I'll Go Where You Want Me To Go" like I did, I knew many were just singing words not realizing what they were saying. It brought tears to my eyes. So let us take a lesson from this and make sure we mean what we sing or say what we mean!

Seeking God

As a young husband and father I had a great hunger for God. My friend, John Martin, was also pressing into God. When he was filled with the Holy Spirit he shouted praises to God out loud and ran around the barn. At times John would come to our farm and we would spend time praying at the feeding entry of the barn by the steer stable. I also remember praying with John in his barn. Many times I would go up in the silo to pray while at other times I would just sit or kneel on the hay bales and pray asking God to move by His Spirit.

When we worked at the Mission Church on Mohn Street in Steelton, Pennsylvania, John was teaching a Sunday School lesson to the adult class, and all of a sudden he turned his head to look to his side, and he said with tears in his eyes "I just heard wings of an angel." Brother John was ordained an elder at Grace Chapel Church. One morning we spent some time together talking about the Lord and the church. When he was leaving my office he turned around and said to me, "If God does not answer one more prayer, I will still serve Him." Now that is commitment!

Habakkuk 3:17-18 says "Although the fig tree shall not blossom, neither shall fruit be in the vines; the labour of the olive shall fail, and the fields shall yield no meat; the flock shall be cut off from the fold, and there shall be no herd in the stalls. Yet I will rejoice in the Lord, I will joy in the God of our salvation."

One of the greatest things for me as a Christian is to be free in my spirit and to stay free. John 8:36 declares that "If the Son therefore shall make you free, ye shall be free indeed." Romans 6:22 and 23 says "But now being made free from sin, and become servants to God, ye have your fruit unto holiness, and the end everlasting life. For the wages of sin is death; but the gift of God is eternal life through Jesus Christ our Lord."

CHAPTER 9 - GOD SPOKE

"Leave the Farm"

In the Spring of 1948, I had bought my first new 1948 8N Ford Tractor which became known as the Red Belly. It served me well on the farm. In June 1955, I was cultivating corn on a beautiful spring morning and God spoke to me in the field, "Leave the farm and go into mission work." I shared this with Edna and together we believed that God was giving us a new direction.

As time came closer to move, we felt a check in our spirits about moving to the Bronx. So as we continued to seek God, we took a trip to Alabama to visit my cousin, David Weaver, and the mission work in the South. We had a very fine trip, but we did not get any leading of the Lord to move to Alabama.

When we returned home, we had one week left until moving day and still did not know where God was leading us. Early the next morning Isaac Burkholder called and offered his small farm house near Annville, Pennsylvania. So we moved there

A recent picture of me praying by a
50 year old 8N Ford Tractor.

where we lived for seven months. In the meantime, Pastor Chester Martin invited us to come and work with them at the Mennonite Mission Church on Sixth & Rilly Street in Harrisburg, Pennsylvania. Now this was the only open door we had left and God gave us peace to move in this direction. We were excited about our new adventure serving our Lord in the inner city and eastern area of Harrisburg. I was assigned to teaching the adult class and Edna was given a girls' class. With our strong Pennsylvania Dutch accent, we served our Lord. One of the Sunday School girls said to Edna, "Can't you talk right?"

Trip to New York City

We became close friends with Rhoda Stolzfus who traveled with us to New York City one weekend. Our 1949 Kaiser had a problem with the door lock, so I knew we could not lock the car. But by mistake someone locked every door and the key we had was not working under any condition. So we had a problem. We couldn't get into the car. Rhoda said, "Please, let me have the key" and with rejoicing in her heart, she crossed to the opposite side of the car. Praying and thanking God, she went to put the key in the lock saying out loud, "In Jesus' name," and unlocked the door. We all rejoiced and thanked the Lord!

Restitution

I took the family to a church in Lebanon, Pennsylvania during a revival meeting. The Evangelist, John Rosenberry, was the preacher. Brother Rosenberry made a comment on our plans to move to New York City. His message that night was on restitution. If you stole, you need to go back and confess it and pay the person the value you stole. Conviction settled in my heart. I remember stealing pencils in the third grade in school and also when John and I stole watermelons at the Martin Zimmerman farm. On a Sunday afternoon years ago John and I went to the Martin Zimmerman farm to visit but no one was at home. However, we noticed that the watermelons there were ripe so John and I took some of them. After we crossed the Cocalico Creek, we broke them open and ate them. Then Brother Rosenberry said "If you shot illegal game you need to confess it." I said in my heart "Yes, Lord, I will make my confession and suffer the consequences."

The very next day at lunch time, there was a knock at the door. Guess who! A game warden. He came to our farm to deliver some safety zone signs to be placed about our building for hunting season. So here was my opportunity. I told him about the call of God on our lives to go into mission work and I wanted to be clear before God and men. Then I confessed to the game warden that a number of years ago I shot twelve pheasants on the first day of hunting season and I desired to have this corrected and whatever he would say or do I would abide by it. The warden was thankful that I acknowledged it but did not wish to fine me under the circumstances. I was thankful to God and was blessed with a new freedom in our precious Lord.

Later I found a member of the Reamstown School Board and made my confession about stealing those pencils. The gentleman forgave me but would not receive my money. I also went to the farmer, Martin Zimmerman, and confessed to him that I had stolen two watermelons when John and I were boys. I tried to pay for them but he forgave me and was thankful for my honesty.

Move to 40th Street

Our stay at Annville was short. The farmer needed the hired hand house for a farm worker. So we began house shopping again. One day while I was out selling W. T. Rawley Home Products since I needed some extra income, I stopped at Hoover's Grocery Store on Derry Street and asked Mrs. Hoover if there were any houses for rent. She told me about Mr. Boyd's house at 215 North 40th Street but quickly warned me, "It's not for rent since the owner was planning to tear it down to build apartments."

About two weeks later I was in the same area and asked a farmer's wife about houses for rent. She smiled and said she was in the grocery store at the time when I asked Mrs. Hoover the same question. Mrs. Markle said "The only house empty in the area is 215 North 40th Street, but it's not for rent." Then I desired to see the owner and was given directions.

I stepped inside the office of the Bonneymead Farms Feed Mill and met a fine tall man my age, Mr. Alex Boyd. After I introduced my self, I asked Mr. Boyd if we could rent the duplex on 40th Street. He clearly and plainly told me that the house was not for rent since he planned in the near future to put apartments in that field. So he did not want to invest any more in the old forsaken place. Now the first time I drove by the house with Edna about two weeks earlier, she would not even get out of the car. The weeds around the porch were about five or six feet tall. The cement walk from the porch to the street was completely invisible because of the weeds. There was nothing attractive about this place. Instead of being persuaded by Mr. Boyd's disinterest, I took a seat in the mill office and proceeded to tell my story. "You see, Mr. Boyd, God has led us to move to the Harrisburg area to help in the Mennonite Mission Church and I'm doing some selling of home products. But I'm also in need of an additional part-time job." Mr. Boyd tilted his hat a bit by scratching his head and said "Do you know anything about farming?" "That's about all I know" was my reply. "Well," Mr. Boyd said, "My farmer got his hand caught in the corn picker a week ago and lost one of his fingers. He won't be able to work for a long time. There are fifteen acres of corn that need to be harvested and the steer stable needs cleaning also. I'm ashamed of the old house since I had fully planned not to let anyone else live in it again because of the future plans of the apartment complex and there is no bathroom." I responded by saying, "Never mind, Mr. Boyd. We don't have a bathroom where we are living now." He then said "If you clean the place up, I'll give you two months free rent and afterwards I'll charge you $20 a month for rent. The reason for the low rent is that I don't want to put any more money into the property. Here is the key, Mr. Weaver. Show it to your family and let me know. You can work on the farm and when the farm work is caught up you can work part time at the feed mill."

I was excited that we had a place to move to and after we cleaned up the place, Edna became happy about the old house. It had no paint. We were thought of as the poor people of the neighborhood. But the truth of the matter was we were the richest people in the whole area because we were sold out to God and God was supplying our needs.

The Mennonite Mission in Harrisburg

We faithfully worked at the Mission Church with Pastor Chester Martin. I became active in visitation and I also transported people in my car to church and Sunday School. We had Pastor Lester Hoover come to be our evangelist. On

The house on 40th Street.

60

Our children on 40th Street.

one of those days, it was arranged that I would go with the evangelist to do house visitation. Everyone we visited that day accepted Jesus as their Saviour and we were so grateful for God's blessing upon us.

In the home of James Harris, Brother Lester asked James if he wanted to receive Jesus as his Saviour. In a very formal way he answered, "Yes sir." Afterwards Brother James Harris became a close friend to me. We did three missionary trips to his hometown in Anderson, South Carolina. Later, he was ordained to the ministry and became the pastor of the Mennonite Church in Anderson.

Precious Years

We had eleven precious years at the old house on 40th Street. The last few years we lived there we had the whole sixteen rooms to ourselves since the neighbor lady moved out of the other side of the duplex after her husband died. So I was planning to take out some walls to make a larger dining room and a larger living room. Well, having a busy schedule, I just didn't get around to it. So one day I came home and found a huge hole in the wall. Edna had taken an ax and put it through the wall. This was her way of helping me to get started. We also put in a very nice bathroom and a clothes closet using the materials that the people gave us.

We had many precious experiences in the old house on 40th Street. A friend, Jean Zimmerman, who recognized that our boys had musical abilities, gave Earl an accordion and we got an old guitar for Mel. Jean gave them lessons. The accordion was a bit heavy for ten year old Earl. Both Mel and Earl learned to play the instruments very well. Earl also learned to play the piano and the organ. We all loved music.

One day, we came home and found Earl and Marty pretending to perform a wedding. They performed the marriage of Tiny, the dog and Charlie, the cat and made a recording of it. When the children would quarrel, Tiny would leave the room. They said, "Tiny was a Christian because he did not like fighting." One day when Tiny got very sick, Edna laid hands on him and asked Jesus to heal him. He immediately was healed and got up and walked away! Our children said, "Why don't we get healed that fast?" Edna answered, "I guess the dog doesn't have any unbelief."

One time Luke, Jr. said, "Daddy, I want a pony." I responded, "Well, I'm sorry I don't have any extra money for a pony, but you can pray and ask the Lord to give you a pony." Many months later a friend of

Luke, Jr. with his pony and homing pigeons.

ours, Farmer Herman Bayshore, felt led of God to give Luke, Jr. a pony. This was his first pony. You see, God answers prayer! Luke, Jr. loved his pony and cared for him and rode the pony often. One winter day he took the pony out on a rope since the pony was not out very often. He could hardly hold him, so he tied the rope around his belly. However, he lost control when the pony started running and dragging him on the snow. The pony ran to the shed and Luke, Jr. was about to hit the wood pile. So he kicked his feet in the snow and was able to swing himself around just enough to miss the pile. He then came in and told the story to his Mom. He only received a scratch from what could have been a serious accident. Praise God for safety! Ginger was Luke, Jr.'s pony for a few years until he sold him for $135. Good business!

"Rats in the Basement" by Edna Weaver

There was an old stone quarry used as a garbage dump about a half block away from our house on 40th Street. Several years after we moved to this house, the township had decided to close the quarry so they filled it with dirt, forcing the rats to leave.

Since no one had lived in our house for a several years, some of the rats from this quarry had moved into the basement. After we moved there, we were surprised to find the rats in the basement where I had stored all our canned vegetables and fruit. While Luke was at work and the children were at school, I would hear the rats in the basement like they were moving my jars. Every time we opened the cellar door we knocked on the door so they would go down into the basement. The ones we saw were quite large.

One morning as Luke and I were having our devotions together (which we always had before he left for work), we could hear a rat trying to work its way up along the pipe under the sink. Now that was too much for me. As long as they were not in the same part of the house that we were, I could endure it. But that morning Luke and I prayed very strong against the devil in these rats. They sure were not a blessing to us.

We rebuked them in the name of Jesus, and asked the Lord to chase them out of our house. Jesus said "Ask anything in my name, and I will do it." So that day the Lord got to work and chased every rat out of the basement. The Lord does all things well. It was so quiet after that day. That was the last of the rats. Our God is able to do exceedingly abundantly above all that we are able to ask or think.

"The Catholic Prayer Meeting" by Edna Weaver

God will fix a fix for you and if you don't get fixed by the fix He fixes for you, He will fix another fix for you! (We first heard this quote from Bob Mumford, a Bible teacher at Elim Bible Institute.)

God will accept you just the way you are, but loves you too much to leave you the way you are. He is so loving. He does

The Mennonite Mission

not condemn you but has ways to open doors for you to walk through to fulfill His blueprint prepared for you before the foundation of the world.

Jeremiah 1:5 - 9 says "I knew you before I formed you in your mother's womb. Before you were born I set you apart and appointed you as my spokesman to the world. 'But Lord, I can't speak. I am afraid of the people.' The Lord replied, Don't say that, for you must go wherever I send you and say whatever I tell you: and don't be afraid of the people, for I will be with you and take care of you!...You will see I have put My words in your mouth." (NLT paraphrased) These verses have helped me through life. The times I felt discouraged, I remembered that God has always thought of us as valuable and that He has a purpose in mind for us!

There were some things we had to overcome before the Lord could use us the way He had planned. The first thing was pride, thinking we were better than others because we had a perfect family of five beautiful children and we all were in church every time the doors were open. Then our youngest son, Luke, Jr., opened our eyes when he turned away from the Lord. Now we realize we had a lot of pride looking down on others thinking if they would train up their children right they would not go astray. We were sure we were doing it right taking our children to church, having family devotions everyday and reading Bible stories at bedtime, etc. But God was dealing with the pride in our hearts.

Second, we had a feeling we were better than the African American people. So God led us to Harrisburg to help with the Mission working with the needy on skid row as well as with the African Americans. It was God's way to teach us that there is no difference in race, color or church background. All people are very valuable to the Lord our God. He died for everyone and it took just as much of the blood of Jesus to cleanse me as it does the worst drunkard in the gutters. So He kept us there until He got our attitudes right.

The third one was the Catholics. We knew we were better

than they were (that is pride,) so He moved us to 40th Street, the same street where the Catholic church was located. This church gave us their left over food from the school lunch and we got a lot of food from them over Thanksgiving, Christmas and Easter.

The Lord put a great hunger in me for a neighborhood Bible study and prayer meeting. So God fixed a fix for me to visit a neighbor lady whom I hardly knew. After I was there a short time another lady came to visit her and soon two more ladies came. Then I was told that today was the day they got together for prayer. I quietly got up to leave but the Lord told me to stay and He reminded me of the promise I had made to do anything He asks me to do. So I asked if it would be all right if I stayed since I never saw anyone pray the rosary. Oh, they were so glad. One of them sat beside me and wanted to give me her rosary. But I said "No, you pray your way and I'll pray my way." Then they showed me the prayer that they were going to be praying that day, the mourner's prayer because a man had died that week. I am embarrassed to tell you that the only prayers I prayed was "Lord, have them ask me to pray so that I can show them the right way." Oh Lord, forgive us of our pride thinking we are better than others.

To my surprise when I left their prayer meeting, the Lord asked me to go back the next week. I thought "Lord, don't you know we don't believe alike?" He said "Didn't you promise me that you'll do anything I ask you to do?" The next week I went back there and as I was getting ready to leave one of the ladies asked me to pray for her mother who lived in New York City and had been ill. The Lord led me to stop and pray right then and there instead of praying on the way home. The next week when I went back again, she told me that she had told her mother how I had prayed for her. She told me that it meant so much to her mother.

In the meantime, this lady had broken her ankle while ice skating with her daughter. Since I was cleaning for others, I said I would help her out. This was God's way of getting me more involved with her. For six weeks I was in her home, cleaning and talking freely and running over with the love of the Lord. So the last time as I was getting ready to leave, she said "If I was not a strong Catholic, you would have me convinced." God's ways are so much higher than our ways. It is the longing in my heart to know Jesus better and to obey when He speaks and to not fear people. My desire is to be a help and a blessing to many more people. It is more of a blessing to give than to receive. God is so good in the bad times and in the good times. He is able to do exceedingly abundantly above all that we can ask or think! May the Lord Jesus bless everyone that is reading our life story!

CHAPTER 10
THE HOLY SPIRIT BAPTISM

Our family in the early 1960's
Front row: Luke and Edna and Luke, Jr.;
Back row: Earl, Mel, Irene, and Marty

On the Seventh Day

Our hunger for God continued. We received prayer for the baptism of the Holy Spirit, first at a home prayer meeting around 1954, and by faith we received the Holy Spirit baptism. Well, that was a step in the right direction. God greatly refreshed us in home prayer meetings at the home of Leon and Ruth Hershey in Paradise, Pennsylvania.

In the summer of 1956, we attended a revival in the Sharon Mennonite Mission in Steeltown, Pennsylvania. Evangelist Clair Shenk was the main speaker. There was a real spirit of revival. Lester and Clarence Ebersole were also used of God in this revival. Lester was the song and worship leader and he was aglow with God's presence, as he led out in worship singing,

"Hallelujah, I have found Him whom my soul so long has sought. Jesus satisfies my longing. By His blood, I now am saved." At times, Lester raised one hand to the Lord as he led worship. He and I became very close friends.

A year later, Lester and his wife, Lois, invited us to a meeting at the home of Norman and Betty Charles on a Thursday night. They also invited Missionary Archie Martin from Ohio. He served as a missionary in Brazil. Archie was anointed of God and full of the Holy Spirit. In this meeting, he was sharing how God was moving by His Spirit in Brazil and also in the States. Near the end, he said, "I see a light coming upon someone," and he came to where I was kneeling and placed his hand upon me. He said, "This light is coming upon this brother. I see this brother preaching before hundreds of people, with an open Bible. I see you ministering with sign gift ministry. I see seven days and God does not tell me what the seven days mean."

This prophecy built faith in me, so Edna and I went on a fast for most of the week and just didn't have a desire for food. The following Wednesday night, I shared the word at the Sharon Mennonite Mission and at the close of the service Edna started to cry and said that she felt like praying all night. She shared this with a few of our friends and Lester and Lois Ebersole came over and joined us after they put their children to bed. It was the four of us in prayer that night. About ten minutes after midnight on the morning of the seventh day which was spoken over me, Lester came and laid his hand upon my head and was praying for me and Jesus baptized me in the Holy Spirit. I felt the power of God flowing through my body, somewhat like the flow of electricity or like the feeling of your arm or leg falling asleep. But it was a very pleasant experience. I started to speak in a stammering tongue, as described in Isaiah 28:11. But very soon I was speaking very fluently in another language. After a time of worshipping God in other tongues, the Spirit gave me the interpretation of tongues and then a prophecy. The Spirit of intercessory prayer then came over me for two and a half hours as I was lying on our living room floor rug. The presence of the Lord was felt and realized by all of us. My baptism of the Holy Spirit was indeed the greatest spiritual experience in all my time since I have been born again.

"Hallelujah! I have found Him whom my soul so long has sought. Jesus satisfies my longing. Through His blood I now am free."

Teaching on the Holy Spirit Baptism

The Book of Acts gives us teachings from God's word on the Holy Spirit baptism. This is what Jesus said in Acts 1:8, "But you shall receive power when the Holy Spirit has come upon you; and you shall be witnesses to Me in Jerusalem, and in all Judea and Samaria, and to the end of the earth." NKJ Acts 2:4 says, "And they were all filled with the Holy Spirit and began to speak with other tongues, as the Spirit gave them utterance." NKJ Acts 10:44-46 goes on to say that "While Peter was still speaking these words, the Holy Spirit fell upon all those who heard the word. And those of the circumcision who believed were astonished, as many as came with Peter, because the gift of the Holy Spirit had been poured out on the Gentiles also. For they heard them speak with tongues and magnify God." NKJ Acts 19:6 says "And when Paul had laid hands on them, the Holy Spirit came upon them and they spoke with tongues and prophesied." NKJ

LOVE

I paraphrased the "love" chapter, I Corinthians 13, as follows. (This was my first writing around 1959.)

"Though I speak with tongues of men and angels and have Love, I become a blessing as the fragrance of the early summer flowers, as the lilacs and honeysuckle, and as tasty as the fresh vegetables from the garden.

"And though I have the gift of prophecy, and understand all mysteries and all knowledge and though I have all faith, so that I could remove mountains and have Love, I become more powerful than the reign of Solomon, for greater than Solomon is here.

"And though I bestow my goods to feed the poor, and though I give my body to the consuming fire (Jesus) and have Love, I shall receive a hundredfold in this life and also eternal life.

"Love endures long and is patient and kind, Love sends out the abundance of peace, Love causes one to speak softly in the presence of wrath, Love boasts in Jesus, Love displays itself humbly, and Love has a sweet desirable countenance about a person.

"Love causes one to behave in a manner so that people will desire to be with you, Love insists not upon its rights but desires its friends to be blessed, Love bears one up sweetly when one is tested greatly, Love thinketh pure thoughts, and Love always rejoices when our friends are blessed spiritually and materially, and when others find the truth.

"Love beareth up in any trial, Love causeth one to believe all the truth that is shown and will continue to seek for more, Love hopeth all things to work out well for his fellowmen, Love endureth all things with sweetness, and Love always causeth one to triumph. Prophecies and tongues are vehicles to bring us unto perfection.

"Love will bring us into the perfect image of Christ. Love will cause our interests to grow from one realm to another, from glory to glory. Love is continually causing us to see greater mysteries of God and will finally allow us to look fully into His wonderful face.

"Real faith is Love in operation. Hope is ourselves entering into the beauty of the Lord, and the greatest of all is Love, for God is Love."

International Bible College

Irene and Melvin were students at the International Bible College (IBC), so I planned to stop and visit them on my way to Mexico. It was a great blessing to see our children and to see the campus on Hallelujah Hill for the first time. While visiting the college, I was privileged to worship with my children at the Sunday service at Revival Temple under the leadership of Pastor John and Ruth Bell. Sister Ruth Bell's father, Leonard Coote, was the founder of IBC. Pastor Bell was raising money for world missions at that time and that year they raised $36,000. As a pastor of a small store front church, I never dreamed of raising that kind of money in a life time. Brother Bell said that next year we are going for $52,000 which was $1,000 a week. I sensed the presence of God very strong and I wept when he made that declaration. I was so thankful that two of my children were blessed to be in such a beautiful spirit-filled church. This is where Grace Chapel Missions was born. Our five children were all students at IBC.

Sister Ruth Bell encouraged everyone to read the Bible daily and to read it through in a year. At the time of this writing I am reading the Bible through for the 32nd time.

"The Singing B's"

In May of 1968, Pastor John Geeseman called me on a Sunday morning and told me about the Singing B's, a teenage girls' trio, Joy Beale, Jeanie Broomell and Judy Craft. I consented to have them come. We praise God for He used them in a great way. They sang,

"My desire is to be like Jesus. My desire to be like Him,
His Spirit fills me, His love o'er whelms me
In deed and word, to be like Him."

The "B's" brought revival and God moved by His Spirit both in the morning and evening services. We invited them to our house for lunch and they all had a great time of fellowship. This was the day Earl met his life companion, "Joy." She is a joy to all of us. This singing group was the forerunner of contemporary gospel singing.

CHAPTER 11
MISSIONARY TRIPS

My First Missionary Trip to Mexico

Jack Hess, Elmer Schich and I took a pickup truck load of clothing to our missionary friend, Melvin High, in South Texas where his mission headquarters is located. Brother High took us over into Mexico to minister. I shall always remember how we drove as far as we could in Brother High's camper and then walked three hours in the night and arrived at our destination about 11:30 PM. When I awoke in the morning, I found myself surrounded by chickens and pigs on the ground floor of the house where we slept!

God blessed our ministry even though we all had dysentery from drinking their water. I had heard that some missionaries had it for three months. I committed myself to the Lord by asking Him to heal me and within 24 hours He healed me!

Melvin and Anna High are doing a great work in Donna, Texas and they are serving many missionaries in Mexico. He is also doing video school of ministry from Gerald Derstine in Mexico in the Spanish language.

Trip to Texas with Mel

In the spring of 1958, I took a trip to Waco, Texas to attend a convention at the Presbyterian Church with Brother Glen Ewing. We went by car with Joe Lehman. I decided to take Mel with me partly because he was a trouble maker and I desired for him to be with me. Melvin seemed to have a mental block. His school teachers were frustrated with him. He brought many books home to study. It was so hard to help him, because it was hard for him to keep his mind on studying. He was twelve years old at the time. It was in this convention when Mel received the baptism of the Holy Spirit. It was not until after this experience that he stopped bringing many books home to do his homework. Edna asked him why he didn't bring books home anymore. Melvin said he didn't need to anymore. Sure enough his next report card showed that he was on the honor roll and he was able to keep his grades up all throughout high school. You see, the baptism of the Holy Spirit broke that mental block. He graduated from high school as a member of the National Honor Society.

First Trip to Florida

In January 1960, Norman and Betty Charles had just sold all their possessions on New Year's Day and were answering the call of God to go to Brazil, South America. They were advised to take a trip to Florida since they had so much illness. Praise God! He healed both of them. They invited us to go with them to Florida. At times on the trip when we stopped to get gasoline, the filling station attendant came under conviction and was in tears as we shared Jesus with him. God blessed the trip and we had many opportunities to share Jesus.

Ben and Marie Mullet had great marital difficulties and God performed a miracle of healing in their marriage. On a Sunday we were invited to their home for a meal. God by His Spirit revealed to me that there was a problem. So I encouraged Ben to lead in a prayer and he just could not do it. I again insisted that he pray and then the miracle happened. He broke down and cried. They fell into each other's arms and cried. God by a miracle restored their marriage that day!

Wesley Ropp was a school teacher in Sarasota, but was skeptical of our freedom and liberty in Christ. When we realized that he had a sinus condition for the last ten years, we laid hands on him and prayed that God would heal him. The phone rang and he took that as an excuse to get away from us. However, while on the phone Wes witnessed to the sales person. After we left, he anointed himself with oil and God completely healed him. At the time of this writing, Wes told me that his healing, which took place 40 years ago, was permanent. We thank God for His grace and mercy!

God supplied the money for this trip to the very last dollar!

CHAPTER 12
THE ANGELS VISIT

The Angel's Appearance to Luke, Jr.

In those days we were seeking God's direction as to where to send our children to school. So the Lord spoke in prophecy through my lips saying, "Send the children to the public school. I will send my angels with them to protect them." The Lord blessed the children in public school. Luke, Jr. won the hearts of the teachers. On one occasion one of them whispered to him, "Tell your Mom I got saved last night."

On December 19, 1961, Luke, Jr. got off the school bus at 40th and Derry Street. Usually he was happy but that day he was concerned about his mother's illness. While he was approaching our house, he heard a voice calling his name. As he looked up, he saw an angel of the Lord in front of our house about four feet above the street standing in mid air. The angel spoke to Luke, Jr. saying "Don't be afraid. Everything will be all right" and then went to the roof top of our house and disappeared into heaven. Luke, Jr. was very excited and came running into the house to his Mom. Edna saw that something unusual happened but wondered if it was good or bad. "Luke, Jr., what happened?" "Mom, I just saw an angel outside and he spoke to me and then disappeared."

Edna had been sick for a number of days. Now, this was during the time when we avoided going to the doctors thinking this would be a dishonor to our Lord and would be a lack of faith on our part. That night as we had family worship, it seemed that the children were a bit discontent and we could not get into unity. I shared a vision that the Lord gave me which indicated the seriousness of Edna's illness. In the vision I saw a hearse coming down 40th Street toward our house. This got everyone's attention and as we were in prayer, Luke, Jr. started to weep like we never heard him weeping before. After a long time of crying he choked out the words and said,

"When I was kneeling by the hassock, Jesus stood by my side." The whole family recognized the presence of the Lord. Edna recovered quickly from her illness, for which we were all so thankful.

December 19th, 2000

On December 19th, 2000, I called Luke, Jr. who lives in New Brunswick, Canada, and asked him, "Please tell your girls that this is the day that you had the angel visitation in 1961." Lisa was twelve years old and the twins, Lyndsey and Loni, were six.

Luke, Jr. was taking his family Christmas shopping at a city about one hour away from their home and was planning to tell the girls about the angel. But before he started, Lyndsey said "Daddy, last night I had a dream. I was walking in the snow and Jesus was walking by my side and a lot of angels were around us." We found it a great blessing when on this same day Lyndsey had this dream of Jesus and the angels walking with her.

Then Luke, Jr. told of his visitation of the angel of the Lord 39 years ago when he was seven years old and in the second grade.

CHAPTER 13
PRAYING IN THE CAPITOL

"The Capitol" By Edna Weaver

God had put a deep hunger in my heart to do anything He asks me to do while I was raising five children on the farm near Ephrata, Pennsylvania. It was during this time that God had put on Gerald Derstine's heart to hold tent meetings near our place. I remember his preaching was good. At the altar call he asked for all of the ones that would promise not to say no whenever God would ask us to do something. I was the first one at the altar.

Some time later as we were touring the Pennsylvania State Capitol building, they were telling us how they never have the front doors locked since it was a practice of the Quakers not to lock the doors but to trust in the Lord and give the Indians food and gifts whenever they came. Because of this, it is on the records that no Quaker was ever scalped or harmed by an Indian.

Edna praying in the House of Representatives at the Pennsylvania State Capitol.

"Obedience to God" By Edna Weaver

On the way home I heard the Lord ask me to go into the Capitol once a week for one hour to pray for the rulers of the Nation. I thought "Never could I do that!" since I was a country girl never getting out among the higher up people. Then the Lord reminded me of the promise I made at the tent meeting to never say no when I am asked to do something. It was then that I knew I must do it or I'd know the rest of my life that I would have disobeyed the Lord because of my natural reasoning and listening to people saying "Can't you pray at home for your rulers?" I said "If God said, go to the Capitol to pray, and I said, I'll do it at home," I would be out of the will of the Lord, and I sure did not want that over my head.

It was around four months until I was willing to obey God. I feel many of us miss out on God's best because our natural mind gets in the way. So right here I want to encourage you to start doing things you have been asked to do like teaching Sunday School, etc. Even if you don't feel capable, remember that this is where God gets the glory. By faith, move ahead and you will be surprised what the Lord will do through you.

After four months I got the strength to go in those big doors of the capitol and walk up to the desk and tell the man that the Lord put it on my heart to come in here once a week to pray for the rulers and asked if that was possible. Now look how the Lord is the best coordinator! The man said, "We are just now ready to get together with a board meeting. I will present it to them, and if you come back in two hours I'll have your answer." So I walked around the grounds praying, remembering that when God is in it all things will work for good. Romans 8:28 declares "And we know that all

The Pennsylvania State Capitol.

Commonwealth of Pennsylvania

The House of Representatives

Citation

Whereas, The Commonwealth of Pennsylvania is always pleased to recognize its citizens who give of their heart and time in the true spirit of concern for others; and

Whereas, Edna Weaver, formerly of Swatara Township, was honored on Christian Heritage Day, April 25, 1990, for praying in the galleries of the Pennsylvania Senate and the House of Representatives for thirty years; and

Whereas, The wife of Pastor Luke Weaver, who founded Grace Chapel in the central Pennsylvania area, Mrs. Weaver attended almost every session of the Legislature for thirty years to pray for the members of both Houses.

Now therefore, the House of Representatives of the Commonwealth of Pennsylvania expresses the deepest appreciation to Edna Weaver in recognition of her thirty years of prayer and inspiration; offers hope that she will continue to live a rich and blessed life;

And directs that a copy of this citation, sponsored by the Honorable Rudolph Dininni on May 4, 1990, be transmitted to Edna Weaver, Route 2, Box 96-A, Bradenton, Florida 34202.

Rudolph Dininni, Sponsor

Speaker of the House of Representatives

Attest:

Chief Clerk of the House of Representatives

Certificate of recognition for Edna.

things work together for good to them that love God, to them who are the called according to his purpose." After their meeting was over, the man said they okayed it if I didn't preach to them. He seemed happy to let me decide where I would like to have my prayer times. He took me all around opening doors so that I could pick any place, the Senate room or House of Representatives, etc.

The first time, I chose the back corner of the House of Representatives but I was too conscious of the large tour groups that came in and saw me sitting there praying. When I came out, the man asked how it was. I asked, "May I go up on the balcony of the House of Representatives?" He said "Sure." From then on, I was taken up there by someone to unlock the door for me. Then when they were in session I watched and prayed.

For one year I was going in there only saying, "Hello" and "Good-bye". Then when Christmas came I gave everyone that took me up on the fourth floor to unlock the door a gift book called *The Cross and the Switchblade* by David Wilkerson. After that I had open doors. Something happened! The Chief of Guards of whom I was afraid because he seemed so mean and looked that way was touched in his heart by the book that I had given him. When he was sick in the hospital and we visited him, he looked at Luke and pointed to me saying "It is all her fault." (He meant that I had led him to know the Lord.) He was so touched that we would come into the hospital to see him. I found out that he was the one that was trying to get a prayer room open for people to come in to pray.

A Catholic man also was touched by God and he said it was because of my witness. Many times I took Luke, Jr. along when he was around eight, nine and ten years old. He would talk with those men and their hearts were always touched by this little boy. Heaven alone will let me know how many got saved because I obeyed the Lord by doing something I did not feel able to do.

"Trust and obey God for there is no other way to be happy in Jesus." Step out in obedience and you will be surprised what the Lord will do. "Souls" is the heartbeat of God.

Pennsylvania State Capitol

Edna being honored with a bouquet of 75 roses for nearly 29 years of praying in the Pennsylvania State Capitol.

According to National Geographic and Smithsonian magazines, "this is the most elaborate Capitol building in the United States." April 29, 1990, was declared by the State of Pennsylvania the first Christian Heritage Day at the State Capitol. We surprised Edna. She was given the official public recognition as the person of greatest honor because she came to the Capitol nearly 29 years to pray for the State and Nation. The biggest bouquet of roses I ever saw, 75 of them, was given to her.

Christmas Tree

At this time in our life, we felt free to put up a Christmas tree in our living room. We decorated it after I put colored lights on the tree. After the family went to bed, I sat on the

Inside the State Capitol.

couch and thanked God for His gift of our Lord and Saviour Jesus Christ. Romans 6:23 says "For the wages of sin is death; but the gift of God is eternal life through Jesus Christ our Lord."

As Edna was going to the State Capitol for prayer usually once a week, she learned that there would be a Christmas tree lighting service in the rotunda of the capitol. So I went to this service with Edna. Lots of people came to the Capitol for this special occasion. We went to the fourth floor balcony to observe the lighting service. As the beautiful Christmas Carols were being sung, God's presence came into the capitol so strong that I found myself weeping. Then I fully realized that God uses Christmas to win souls. Later I learned that during this service, a friend of ours, Charlie, was watching this program on television and his living room filled up with a supernatural light of God's presence.

"Not So Much Doing But Being" By Edna Weaver
(A copy of Edna's first tract)

As children of God, we not only have been called, we are not only one of God's children, but we are called to be bound (deeply devoted) to the Lord.

What does it mean to be bound to the Lord Jesus Christ? It's giving up our rights, and becoming a servant, one that is held in captivity by his master.

Jesus, of His own accord, laid aside His rights and position as Son of God and became a man. "But made Himself of no reputation,...and was made in the likeness of men" Philippians 2:7.

"As He is, so are we in this world" I John 4:17(c).

We are not necessarily called to "doing" but rather to "being" what God wants us to be. "For though I be free from all men, yet have I made myself servant unto all, that I might win them to Christ" I Corinthians 9:19. We are only to be useable and led by God if we want to bless many others. Only when our eyes have turned away from our own works will we become ready and willing to be led by the Lord, allowing Him to work through us. If we are honestly being a servant, then we must be ready for that "special calling" the Lord has for each of His children.

But first, we must prove ourselves in the "general calling." "Then said Jesus unto His disciples, if any man will come after Me, let him deny himself, and take up his cross, and follow Me" Matthew 16:24.

A good soldier will not rush out to battle until he has been trained and sent. We, as servants of God, must not move until we hear from our Head, the Lord Jesus Christ. Many times there is a time of waiting, a period of quiet time when we are set apart to wait for a more special ministry.

"During this time, God will fix a fix for you. And if you don't get fixed by the fix he fixes for you, God will fix another fix to fix you!" – Bob Mumford

If we accept this waiting time as a time of preparation, God will then move us into that special calling.

"For since the beginning of the world men have not heard, nor perceived by the ear, neither hath the eye seen...what He hath prepared for him that waiteth for Him" Isaiah 64:4. "...My meat is to do the will of Him that sent me, and to finish His work" John 4:34. "As He is, so are we in this world!" I John 4:17(c). These two callings are different.

Do you find within yourself the "deep calling unto the deep" Psalm 42:7? If so, be careful. Do not become over anxious and rush out before you are sent out by God. There are many who went out before God's timing, only to become hurt more than necessary. This deep inner sense of "being called" is only a signal for us to be alert to His still small voice telling us what He wants our next step to be. We must first learn our place as a servant and wait for further instructions.

Yes, there may be hard times of preparation, so we must pull back on the reins of our inner man that wants to run ahead and avoid the time of preparation. To run ahead of our time of service would only be asking for failure and the soon-fainting of our spiritual man. Time is a very precious thing if we keep in step with the Master. Seeing a need does not constitute a sending forth.

We must learn to do as Jesus did. He did nothing unless the Father showed Him. (John 5:19) The sooner we submit to the will and leading of God and remain faithful to Him, the sooner we will find ourselves placed into that higher calling. "I press toward the mark for the prize of the high calling of God in Christ Jesus" Philippians 3:14.

If we could look back, we would see the path crowded with "hoped-to-be-experts and success seekers" who, with secret envy, turned their eyes away from Jesus and got their eyes on their calling. They saw those who had laid down their very lives and made themselves of no reputation in fulfilling their special callings and they longed to be like them. They wanted great results in their ministry but were not willing to go through the time of preparation to pay the price.

They never came to that place of God's highest, because they could not honestly pay the price of being a servant, giving up their personal rights. So they were filled with disappointments ...not in their salvation, but in their ministry. They did not become what they had hoped to be or even what they thought God called them to be. They were not willing to take up their cross and become a servant.

If we are faithful in the general calling of denying ourselves, then God will move us into the special calling - that ministry which is His heart's desire for each of His children. "Many are called, but few are chosen."

The greatest need in the church is not more pastors, teachers, evangelists, or prophets, but those who will be faithful, useful vessels in which the Father can portray His image.

There is no change without pain. Nothing produces depression faster or more deeply than self pity!

"Those who bring sunshine to the lives of others can not keep it from themselves." (Source unknown)

May God the Father and Christ Jesus our Lord shower you with His kindness, mercy and peace.

I want to remind you to stir into flame the strength and boldness that is in you! For the Holy Spirit, God's gift, does not want you to be afraid of people, but to be wise and strong, and to love them and enjoy being with them.

If you will stir up this inner power you will never be afraid to tell others about our Lord. Hold tightly to the pattern of truth, especially concerning the faith and love Christ Jesus offers you.

Guard well the splendid God-given ability you received as a gift from the Holy Spirit who lives within you.

Oh, Father, give us men and women who are willing to go step by step into that high calling! "For though ye have ten thousand instructors in Christ, yet have ye not many Fathers; for in Christ Jesus I have begotten you through the Gospel" I Corinthians 4:15.

Lord, help us to be among the faithful ones! Show us your way, O Lord.

CHAPTER 14
A BURDEN FOR THE CITY

City of Harrisburg

I went to the Reservoir Park one day to pray. While I looked over the city praying and interceding, I asked God to give us the key to revival for the city. I was so hungry for the outpouring of the Holy Spirit for our city and we wanted souls to be saved. During this time Edna and I along with our children went to visit some neighbors. We prayed for them and were a spiritual strength to them. Now 40 years later, Life Center, a charismatic church, purchased property for their church and outreach center. This property just so happened to be the home of these neighbors whom we visited and to whom we spent some time ministering!

The Friday Night Prayer Meeting

A group of families gathered together for a Friday night prayer meeting and service in various homes. I became the leader of this group. It was from this group that Grace Chapel was birthed. One of the families, a farmer Enos Hess, told us that when strawberry season came, "I want you to come and pick all the strawberries you need free of charge." He gave them to us as a gift to the Lord. After that there was a killing frost that froze many of the strawberry blossoms which caused the strawberries in that area to have a very short crop. But God protected the Hess crop and the frost did not harm their berries. Praise the Lord!

God promised that if we bring "all the tithes into the storehouse,... and prove Me now herewith, saith the Lord of Hosts, if I will not open you the windows of heaven, and pour you out a blessing, that there shall not be room enough to receive it. And I will rebuke the devourer for your sakes, and he shall not destroy the fruits of your ground" Malachi 3:10-11a.

Gospel Signs

Why is it dangerous to throw stones at a gospel sign? When we moved to 40th Street in Harrisburg I put gospel signs on each side of the mail box. The signs quoted Matthew 11: 28-29 "Come unto me, all ye that labour and are heavy laden, and I will give you rest. Take my yoke upon you, and learn of me; for I am meek and lowly in heart; and ye shall find rest unto your soul." Across the street I had a larger sign quoting Isaiah 55:6 "Seek the Lord while He may be found; call upon Him while He is near." NKJ

One day the sign across the street was torn down and broken. Some time after this a neighbor man came to our store front church on Derry Street and we ministered to him. After I got acquainted with this neighbor, I invited him to go with me to a speaking engagement in New York State. His testimony was that he had a business loss and also some major marital problems and he became very depressed. So he took a walk in the neighborhood trying to overcome his depression and gloom. His walks took him past our house and he did not like those gospel signs. In trying to overcome his frustration, he threw stones at the gospel signs. Well, that was not good enough so he broke down the signs and threw them across the street in the wooded area.

Thank God, he got saved! And the mystery of "who broke the gospel signs" was solved.

Bumper Sticker

I put "Christ is the Answer" on the trunk of my car in red neon stripes. That was before bumper stickers were invented.

We Shared

We shared our new found blessing of the baptism of the Holy Spirit wherever we could. Some of our friends and relatives listened and thought we had gone off the deep end (fanatical). One of my cousins came to correct me concerning this "false doctrine" that I had gotten into. Through the gift of prophecy, the Lord told us beforehand that when they came to bring correction that I should not argue. He said "Don't argue." I took this to heart and when my cousin came, I listened and then I said to him, "Keep on praying for us. We only want God's best."

About one year after we received the Holy Spirit baptism, we felt led of the Lord to leave the church. So I talked to my Bishop, Wilman Strong, and told him that we were leaving the church. Brother Strong said, "We need you here. Why will you leave?" "Well, we can't be free here." "In what area can't you be free?" "In the gifts of the Spirit." "What gifts?" "The gift of tongues." Brother Strong was precious and said, "I never told you that you can't speak in tongues." Leaving our beloved church was a difficult move because it brought on some rejection. However, we started going to Charlotte Street Church in Lancaster for about one year.

Mohn Street

In the old town hall where the glory of the community had been departed for many years, the opportunity came for us to start a Sunday school and worship service. With the help of John and Mary Martin, we began this project in April 1959. Some of our friends from the country came to give us moral support and worship with us. We were able to get a nice group of children to come on Sunday morning but no adults from the area came. However, we had the blessing to minister to the adults on Tuesday nights.

One Tuesday night, Mrs. Kent who had a nervous breakdown heard us sing and was led to come to the meeting. She could not sleep or eat and was not feeling safe to be left alone. As we worshipped God and prayed, Jesus completely healed her. She was so happy. The dark cloud of gloom that was over her was gone and she shouted out, "I can see light!" Praise God!

Whenever we visited the home of Sister Sprigg, her aged father always quickly disappeared. He just did not want to see us. So one day as she was telling of her daddy's bad heart condition, I asked her for one of his white handkerchiefs and I prayed over it and anointed it with oil in the name of Jesus according to Acts 19:11. Then I told her to put it under her daddy's pillow so he would be lying on it whenever he would lie down. The next time we came to her house her daddy met us at the door and was so happy to see us. Jesus healed him and now he enjoyed our visit whenever we would come see them.

Norman Charles off to Brazil

I went with Norman to Philadelphia to get his visa to go to Brazil. While we were in Philadelphia, we wanted to be a witness for our Lord, so we decided on a plan on Market Street since it was a busy street. While Norman was on one side of the street and I was on the other side, he called out real loud, "What must I do to be saved?" I answered from across the street, "Believe on the Lord Jesus Christ and thou shall be saved." I'm not sure that this method worked but we had lots of joy trying it. You guessed right! Our wives were not along. They would have been embarrassed by us.

By March of 1960, we saw Norman and Betty Charles off to Brazil. They sailed from New York City. We had taken a bus load of people to see them off on the big freighter which carried only a few passengers. Before they departed, I stood up on a barrel and gave them a farewell address.

In 1961, we had a convention in the Montimental Baptist Church. God blessed and we started a car fund for Norman Charles' missionary work in Brazil. It was here that I met my close friend Ed Maurer. Brother Ed is a soul winner and has led many people into the baptism of the Holy Spirit. Gerald Derstine was the main speaker at this convention.

Aircraft

In 1958, I was running a delivery truck with eggs and produce going from door to door. I saw a large aircraft flying over that day. It was large enough to carry one army tank or about six jeeps at one time. As I watched this huge airplane, I realized that this plane was designed to fly. This plane had four big turboprop motors with plenty of power to put it into flying speed. I saw this as an illustration of our Christian life. After we are saved, we fly as with eagles' wings. Isaiah 40:31 says "But they that wait upon the Lord shall renew their strength; they shall mount up with wings as eagles; they shall run, and not be weary; and they shall walk, and not be faint."

If I can illustrate, the earth represents the sinful nature, and the skies represent flying in victory. As long as the airplane has power, it can fly; and as long as we walk in God's Spirit and in God's will, we can keep mounting up with wings as eagles.

1 Corinthians 15:57 "But thanks be to God which giveth us the victory through our Lord Jesus Christ." We thank God for the blood of our Lord Jesus.

1 John 1:7 "But if we walk in the light, as He is in the light, we have fellowship one with another, and the blood of Jesus Christ His Son cleanseth us from all sin."

Romans 6:18 "Being then made free from sin, ye become the servants of righteousness."

Romans 6:20 " For when ye were the servants of sin, ye were free from righteousness."

Romans 6:22 "But now being made free from sin, and become servants to God, ye have your fruit unto holiness, and the end everlasting life."

Romans 6: 23 "For the wages of sin is death; but the gift of God is eternal life through Jesus Christ our Lord."

As we press into God we can overcome the world, the flesh and the devil, because we are learning to know Him and the power of His resurrection.

Temptations

Years ago I often wondered why Bill Gothard called his teaching seminars "Basic Youth Conflicts" even though his audiences consisted of people of all ages. I realize later in life that the temptations the middle age or older persons face are basically the same except that they have a bit different flavor. Galatians 5:16 exhorts us to "walk in the Spirit, and ye will not fulfill the lust of the flesh." This word is speaking to the believers. It indicates that the believers will have temptations and struggles. Galatians 5:18 says "but if ye are led of the Spirit, ye are not under the law."

It is a common thought that when a person gets older, they get more holy. This is not correct. Earlier in life I was hired by a public works department to do highway construction work and at another time I worked as a carpenter building houses. Some of the older men that I worked with had filthy mouths.

It is only the blood of Jesus that cleanses us from all sin!

Baby Paul

In 1960 when Norman Charles went to Brazil, we went with family and friends on the school bus to New York City's seaport to see them leave. It was right after that trip that Edna was having some complications with her four and a half months pregnancy. She was hemorrhaging a lot. We had Dr. Pilgram come to the house. He examined her and determined that the baby had passed. But after the doctor left, Edna became very ill and then the baby passed. I saw that it was a little boy and that same night I buried the baby on our property.

Edna was so ill from losing too much blood. She was near death's door. I earnestly prayed and fought a battle between life and death. As the sun rose the next morning, Edna miraculously received new strength. When the doctor came again to the house about ten o'clock that morning, Edna was sitting up in bed. It seemed like God gave her a blood transfusion. We praise our God for raising her up again to health!

CHAPTER 15
THE BIRTH OF GRACE CHAPEL

Basement Church

On Sunday morning of September 25, 1962, we moved our services into the basement of Charles and Eileen Fetter's house where the birth of Grace Chapel took place. Approximately 50 to 60 people were present. Our regular people were eight families with attendance of 42 people.

God was ministering to us through His word. I preached with great excitement. Earl played the accordion, Mel played the guitar, Charles Fetter played the electric guitar and Sister Eileen played the organ. Lester Bowman was our first song leader. God was meeting our spiritual needs. About the second year of the service, Charles McKeen was amazed at my energetic type of preaching. He said that I was all over the place. He was skeptical of me, so he silently prayed and said, "If that preacher is for real have him come over and pray for me." Charles was suffering with some pain in his cheek. As soon as he prayed that silent prayer to the Lord, I stopped preaching and walked back up the aisle and laid my hand on him and prayed for him. Well, we have been friends ever since and he took me to the airport on many missionary trips until he went to heaven in December 1993. Thank you, Charles.

The Store Front Building

One Sunday morning when the Fetters were away on a trip, Luke, Jr. and Ken Martin went to the Doberman pinscher watchdog and were petting the dog. Just as Ken walked away the dog attacked Luke, Jr., biting him on the head and leaving his eyelid torn open, his nose injured and a cut about one inch long just above his hair line. Well, needless to say, this was of great concern so he was rushed to the hospital to be treated and sewn up. He recovered speedily. It was then that we decided it was time to look for a building.

We moved to a storefront building on 6530 Derry Street where God opened doors for us to bring in many of the well known speakers of the charismatic movement. Dr. Jack Herd would bring them in for the Full Gospel Business Men's meetings and I would have them at church on Sunday mornings or nights. When we heard of the Cameron Family from Scotland, we invited them there. They brought the joy of the Lord with them and we packed out the little Derry Street Church with 260 people that day. People came from far and near to get the blessing that God was pouring on us. The Camerons were a great blessing to us. Simon Cameron said:

"The British love the Gospel, because they can talk about it.
The Irish love the Gospel, because they can fight about it.
The Welsh love the Gospel because they can sing about it.
The Scotch love the Gospel because it is free."
Pastor Joe Crandall and Pastor Mel Courey came to our Store Front Church and brought God's presence and glory with them, but they said that we brought the Spirit of God's blessing to them.

Grace McKeen

Grace McKeen was brought back from heaven after a cerebral hemorrhage and a massive stroke. On the way to the hospital, the paramedics called the hospital and said that this woman will live about ten minutes.

Grace was in a coma for four days. A 24 hour prayer chain was formed. One of our friends, Wayne Stoner, put a tape player in her room for her to listen to Bible reading to strengthen her by the continual reading of God's word. She later told us that she could hear at all times.

Jesus came and asked Grace to go with Him. As she went through the dark tunnel, the valley of the shadow of death, she could hear the voice of Jesus saying, "You can make it. Look for the light at the end of the tunnel." She then saw the beautiful pearly gates and they were opening a little at a time.

She could see far into the brilliant celestial city. Through the gate of the City of Light she heard voices of children laughing and playing and waves of beautiful music coming out to her. Seeing all that brilliant beauty, she wanted to go through the gate into heaven but Jesus told her three times "I must send you back. Scott needs you." Her son, Scott, was fourteen years old and claiming the promise of God in Ephesians 6:1-3 "Children, obey your parents in the Lord, for this is right. 'Honor your father and mother,' which is the first commandment with promise: 'that it may be well with you and you may live long on the earth.'" NKJ Scott had said, "Mom is only 53 years old and I want her to come back and be made whole, because Mom has always been obedient to her parents. God, you owe her some more time."

Looking back to earth, Grace saw her body on the hospital bed in a paralyzed condition and said "Jesus, if You send me back I want a normal healthy body to live in. That one does not move or talk. I need a body that will praise You."

On the following morning which was Easter Sunday, I went early to the hospital to give Grace communion if she could receive it. I said "Grace, how are you today?" Grace answered for the first time and said "Good!" "Oh, you can talk now!"

She could only speak words and had to learn to put sentences together. It was Scott's prayer and standing on the Scriptures that Jesus sent her back. Grace is still alive and well after 28 years!

Water Baptism

Before we had the baptistery, we had water baptism services in Zerby's farm pond. God's Spirit was so precious. Lonnie McKeen (Grace McKeen's daughter) was the first person to be baptized there. When we baptized her, she went out in the Spirit. So we had to carry her out to the grassy bank. Another friend of ours, Estel Waidlich, at the age of 70 was also touched by God while she was being baptized in water. We had to float her out and put her on the grassy bank. Many

Water baptism at Mount Union, Pennsylvania.

others were baptized there.

We became involved in water baptism at the Jesus Ministry. We also became involved in water baptism at the Full Gospel Businessmen's Fellowship Annual Convention with Dr. Jack Herd, the president, for many years.

I taught on water baptism and we baptized many people, and many had spiritual experiences with our Lord Jesus.

The scriptures command us to be baptized in water according to Matthew 28:18, Mark 16:16, Acts 2:38 and Acts 19:5. The Bible teaches us that salvation is by grace through faith. (Ephesians 2:8 & 9) But more can happen in water baptism.

According to Acts 2:38, we have repentance and remission of sins. Romans 6:3 teaches baptism into Jesus Christ. This is becoming fully identified with Him. Romans 6:6 goes on to say that our old nature is buried in water baptism. Verses 11 & 12 of Colossians 2 explain that heart circumcision is connected with water baptism. I Peter 3:21 tells us that there is cleansing of the conscience toward God at baptism.

The House of the Lord

In 1973, I received a phone call from Linda and David Stoltzfus. They had a prayer fellowship in their home in Mechanics Grove, Pennsylvania. They needed help and wanted teaching on casting out demons. We went to many of the Thursday night prayer meetings and were able to assist them. Many people were helped and young people were set free from the power of Satan and sinful habits. The local pastor did not understand and rejected the move of the Spirit of God.

When David and Linda were baptized in our store front chapel in Harrisburg, their lives were changed and God brought them into a new liberation in Christ. David and Linda are now pastoring The House of the Lord in Willow Street, Pennsylvania. Linda said that we were a jump start to them.

The Worship Center

Sam and Sherlyn Smucker were members of the prayer group in Mechanics Grove. Ken Sauder and Sam came to us in Harrisburg to receive counsel about deliverance. I told them that they should not be demon conscious, but keep Jesus first in the ministry. And if the need arises to cast out demons, we need to take care of it, but go on lifting up Jesus (Mark 16:16).

Sam and Sherlyn pioneered and are now pastoring the Worship Center in Leola, Pennsylvania. It is a large and powerful work in Lancaster County.

The Lord's House of Prayer

Mark and Abby King were members of the Mechanics Grove Prayer Group. Mark reminded us recently that we had come about once a month to this prayer group for a good part of a year, and said that I was their spiritual guide and mentor, like a special model father to them.

Their water baptism was a spiritual high. When this couple was being baptized in the baptismal tank at Derry Street, a prophecy came forth for them to go to Russ Bixler Bible School.

Now they are pastoring the Lord's House of Prayer in Lancaster, Pennsylvania.

David Hess

We met David before he and Sherri were married. As a young man, David got fascinated with the occult and got involved in it. He read the satanic bible. Through this he got a spirit of terror and fear and could not sleep. At that time David had not heard about the Holy Spirit. Sherri and her family brought him to a Full Gospel Businessmen's Convention in Harrisburg, Pennsylvania. David had the desire to be free from his bondage. As we were praying for him, I discerned by the Holy Spirit that he had a spirit of terror. David received some help that day, but they came to the Store Front Church for further help. The demonic activity was so strong that he felt an invisible demonic force pulling him off the couch where he was sitting.

We gave him some basic teachings from Mark 16:16 which promises us that in Jesus' name we shall cast out demons, John 8:32 "And you shall know the truth and the truth shall make you free," (NKJ) John 8:36 "if the Son makes you free, you shall be free indeed," (NKJ) and Acts 10:38 "How God anointed Jesus of Nazareth with the Holy Ghost and with power: Who went about doing good, and healing all that were oppressed of the devil; for God was with Him."

After we prayed a simple but powerful prayer with authority, David was completely set free from all demonic activities. We are thankful to the Lord for this. We stood upon Psalm 91:11 "For He shall give His angels charge over you, to keep you in all your ways." NKJ

In January 1976 we baptized David in water at Grace Chapel on Derry Street and God gave him a complete liberation in Christ. David and Sherri are now pastoring the Christ Community Church in Camp Hill, Pennsylvania.

Mike Warnke

Mike and Susan Warnke.

In 1975 I first heard the author of Satan Seller. Mike Warnke had met the Lord while in military boot camp. We had the opportunity to have him in our home and to speak in our church. He also spoke at the Full Gospel Businessmen's meeting where 1,000 people had attended. After spending about six days at our house, he asked if he could adopt us as his parents. His parents had died and he was an orphan. He had a desire to have Christian parents. We and our children agreed to this, but he chose to keep his own name. The Lord said that Warnke was close enough to the name Weaver. He met my mother and Edna's mother and was well received by them.

We enjoyed his ministry and he enjoys coming to our house and having mom's good cooking. Mike has been part of our family for 25 years.

Demos Shakarian

I met Demos Shakarian in Park Sheesley's cow barn. As Park was showing Demos his very expensive top breed Holsteins this one late Sunday afternoon, I said, "Demos, will you please come to our church and give our folks a few minutes of greetings?" Well, it so happened that about 8:55 that evening the front door of the Chapel opened and Demos, Park and Irene came in. As Demos started his greeting, the Holy Spirit impressed him that he should give his testimony. So the few minutes turned into one hour and God renewed Demos' strength. From that time on, we became personal friends.

Enoch Christoffeson called me from Terlock, California and said, "We need your witness on the trip to the Orient." I promised him that I would pray about it. The following Sunday morning as I was up early at the Store Front Church, I knelt in prayer and asked the Lord if He wanted me to go on the Full Gospel Airlift to the Orient and God spoke to my heart and said, "I want you to go."

Near Plane Accident

About a week later, a sister from our greater community said that she had a revelation that she saw our plane crashing into the Pacific Ocean and everyone was killed. Well, I thought that was interesting because the Lord by his Spirit told me to go. I guess I bargained a bit with God. "God, since you told me to go to Japan and the Orient I'm asking you to give us a safe round trip missionary journey." Thank God, He did!

As we were getting ready to land in Korea, our pilot decided that he needed to pass the airport and make a U-turn in order to come in from the other direction. Apparently the pilot was in a hurry and had cut the corner and did not fly out as far as he should have. It was a 204 passenger DC8 Stretch Jet and every seat was filled. As the pilot was landing the plane and slowing down, the plane started sliding. My friend, Paul, was a pilot of a small aircraft. He said that he nearly screamed out loud when he felt the DC8 sliding. The pilot quickly put on what seemed like full power. He did this twice and then I felt the wheels touching the runway, but now at a much faster speed than in normal landings.

Praise God! He saved us from that crash that Satan had planned for us. This incident has built my faith to trust God for safety on air flights or any travels. Miraculously, God not only protected us but also supplied the money to pay for this trip.

CHAPTER 16
THE MIRACLE AT SHARON VILLAGE

Claudio Cortez

Before we flew over to the Philippines, we stopped in Cosa Mesa, California, and visited Demos at the Headquarters Building of the Full Gospel Businessmen's Fellowship International. When we arrived at the Manila Airport in the Philippines, I said to my friend, Paul, "Gerald Derstine has a contact here in the Philippines. Where is it?" Paul answered, "That is where we are going." A few hours later we landed in Tuguegarao, Cagayan. The

Hosanna and Claudio Cortez

welcome was outstanding as the believers sang to us as we entered Sharon Village. The rains were so heavy that the planned meetings for Friday and Saturday nights were canceled because the roads were washed out. So we had meetings in a small building at Sharon Village. We gave testimony and shared the word of God. The Filipinos sang and praised God. I said to myself, "Must I go half way around the world to get my soul blessed?" I believe that we laid hands on and prayed for every one there.

On Sunday morning we were taken to a young man that was very sick and we prayed for him. It seemed like he was almost unconscious. I laid my hand on him and prayed but realized that he could not understand English. I asked the Lord to lay His hand upon him and heal him. After prayer, Paul and I asked him to rise like the crippled man in Acts

Welcome at Sharon Village.

chapter three and we walked him over to the church service that had already started. Brother Cortez had him give his testimony. People were rejoicing and Brother Cortez was crying.

A few weeks after we returned home, Brother Claudio Cortez, the native pastor, wrote me a letter. He said that everyone in those meetings who was not saved became born again. There were eighteen miraculous healings and 42 people received the Holy Spirit baptism. In the letter, he stated that the man who was prayed for testified that while the two missionaries were praying for him, a beautiful white hand came and touched him and he was completely healed from all sicknesses. This was the first outpouring of the Holy Spirit at Sharon Village. Two of the brothers could only speak in tongues for seven days. They could not speak their own native language. A white dove flew around in the church auditorium. The students saw flames of fire in the church and they were leaping up to touch the fire. Brother Cortez said he had to dismiss the students because they were so full of God's power that they could not study. So he sent them home for a week.

When they all came back, everyone of them reported that they had won people to the Lord.

The believers at Sharon Village kept praying for us to return. Seven years later Edna and I went and God blessed our ministry with them. Believers were strengthened and souls were saved.

On a later trip, Joe and Clara Dailey went with us on a crude boat to cross a river into a village where we then rode on an ox cart. We had open air meetings and a church was started as a result.

On one of the trips we were riding the Land Rover to go for some distance to minister. The vehicle broke down right in front of a house in the countryside. There was a man in the house that I wanted to lead to Jesus. They told me there's a problem. He cannot hear. So I laid hands on him and asked Jesus to heal him. Praise God! His ears opened up and he could hear. So I was then able to lead him to Jesus.

On a later trip I asked Claudio Cortez, Jr. to take me to town for some ice cream on his motorcycle. So I took the opportunity to share with him and encouraged him to come to Christian Retreat to the Institute of Ministry. God touched him and that day as we were eating ice cream, he made a decision to give up studying for business and to prepare to go into the ministry with his daddy. He did go into the ministry and has become very effective.

DC-10 Jumbo Jet

Edna and I left Manila, Philippines to return to the USA. The ten hour flight to Hawaii took us over the international date line. A businessman was sitting just across the isle from us. After the dinner meal was served I engaged him in conversation.

While in Hawaii, we bought some Hawaiian clothing. My shirt matched Edna's dress. This businessman asked me if we were Mennonites. I asked him why he asked me this question. He replied "Well, I saw you have a Bible." We learned then that he went to Eastern Mennonite College in Harrisonburg,

Learning to eat with chopsticks in Taiwan.

Virginia. Thank God I was able to speak into his life and be a witness to him. When I told him that we were going to Salem, Oregon to see our daughter, Marty, he asked me if I would call his father and tell him that the business trip was successful. Just before we went to the airport in Oregon to come home, I remembered that I needed to call his father who was a Mennonite preacher. As I talked with this preacher it seemed like he was very distant and inexpressive, so he asked me again "Who did you say you are?" "I'm Pastor Luke Weaver from Harrisburg, Pennsylvania. We are here in Oregon visiting my daughter." He said "I had a friend named Luke Weaver but he died." I guess he thought he was hearing from his dead friend. He then told me that he appreciated that I was able to speak into his son's life.

CHAPTER 17
TESTIMONIES OF HEALING

Accident

We were on the way to a house meeting and we came to an accident. A boy on his bicycle was hit by a delivery truck and was lying on the road unconscious and bleeding from his temple. At each heartbeat the blood gushed out like a geyser. He could only live for a few minutes in this condition. I remembered the word in Ezekiel 16:6 which says "And when I passed by thee, and saw thee polluted in thine own blood, I said unto thee when thou was in thy blood, 'Live!'" I laid my hand upon him and prayed in the name of Jesus, "You are polluted in your blood and you shall live" and instantly the blood stopped. We waited until the ambulance came. They took him to the hospital.

Some weeks later I stopped at his house, and the boy was perfectly well. So I told the mother about the bleeding and how the Lord had stopped the blood. They were thankful that God had healed their son.

Boy Healed of Bad Eyesight

I was invited to preach in a church near Erie, Pennsylvania. The pastor's son who was about 12 years old was not doing well in his lessons at school. The school nurse checked his eyes and found the reason for his failing. So she sent word to the parents to have the boy fitted with glasses.

This family was trusting God for a miracle. This boy came to me for prayer so that God would heal his eyesight. The next day when he went to school he told the school teacher that the Lord Jesus had healed him. So they examined his eyesight again, and praise God, his eyesight was found to be normal and he did not need glasses.

Man in a Coma

Edna and I got a call to pray for a man on his death bed. At the time, he was in a coma. The wife was so concerned about his salvation because he had not committed himself to Christ. Now at this time there was no evidence that the man could hear or understand us. However, I felt led to talk to him as if he could hear me. So I asked him to say in his spirit that he acknowledges His sins and to say in his heart that Jesus died and rose again so that he could be saved. I prayed and committed him to God and asked Jesus to wash his sins away.

The wife was asking God to give her a sign that her husband was going to heaven. About a week after the time of prayer, this man who was in a coma smiled and then slipped out of his body and died. The wife was so thankful now that she had the assurance that her husband went to heaven.

The Healing of Ralph Rudy

One evening I had a call to pray for Ralph Rudy. Ralph was in the Pola-Clinic Hospital in Harrisburg, Pennsylvania. He just had an operation that removed most of the stomach. His fever went over 106 and they put him on ice packs. The doctors told the family that they should get a minister. As I came into the hospital room with his wife and daughter, I remembered how God raised up a very sick man in the Philippines. I prayed in my heart, "Will You please do it in Harrisburg like You did it half way around the world?" So I shared this testimony and asked them to believe God with me for a miracle.

His wife and daughter were watching him while I was praying, and they said that half way through the prayer his color came back into his face. He slept that night and the next morning he said he was hungry. He was soon released from the hospital and when he was brought home, he was so hungry that he asked his wife to make him beefsteak and he ate a full meal for a healthy person. God must not only have healed his stomach but restored it to normal size. The next

Sunday they were all at church filling up two church benches. Praise God!

Full Gospel in Huntington, Pennsylvania

I was the guest speaker at the dinner meeting of the Full Gospel Businessmen's Fellowship International in Huntington, Pennsylvania. Darrell Shawver was the chapter president. I took along with me, Edna, Earl and Joy and her new singing group called The Challengers. They ministered in songs and I gave a testimony and preached. At closing I felt led of the Holy Sprit to minister to a number of people with certain illnesses. By the word of knowledge, I called out about ten different needs and asked the people to respond if it was their need. I waited and no one responded. I thought to myself, I guess I missed it. But as we waited a little longer one person got up and said, "That was me." Then another until God had healed everyone to whom the word of knowledge pertained. We were so thankful for the goodness and the faithfulness of our God.

CHAPTER 18
HAITI

Bishop Joel Jeune

My cousin, Bill and Darlene Martin, took Edna and me to Haiti for the first time in 1968. On our third trip, we helped ordain a few of the men to help Bishop Joel Jeune. They started a small church and a Christian school. I asked Pastor Joel why he did not have a feeding program in his school. His answer was because he did not have the money to do so. So I spoke to many of my friends here in the USA and we raised the monthly support for the school and the feeding program.

On one of our earlier mission trips to Haiti, Pastor Joel and his wife, Doris (nicknamed Guerly), took us to the Mountain of Savane Zombie to Papa Rameau, Joel's father. This was a distance of 65 miles but much of the road was very bad.

Our first flat tire was about 20 miles into our trip. I asked Pastor Joel, "Where are the four new inner tubes that I

Bishop Joel and Doris Jeune

brought along from Pennsylvania." He said, "They are back at our house. I forgot to bring them." Well, it so happened that our flat happened by the Mennonite Missionary's house. So they gave us tube patches and let us use their jack, lug wrench and the tire irons and the tire pump.

So as we traveled these rough roads, mountains and more mountains, there were times when some of the men walked because they could walk faster than the truck was going. After four flat tires and thirteen hours, we arrived at our destination. The people were so happy to see us. We were the first white people that some of them had ever seen. Joel's father pioneered 35 churches in the mountains of Haiti. Both of Joel's parents are in heaven.

When Joel was about two years old, he was very sick with dysentery. His father prayed and committed him to the Lord and went on his horse to go preaching. Instead of getting better, little Joel died. Some of the men made a little coffin in preparation for burial the next day. They do not embalm the bodies so they needed to bury him as soon as possible.

There was no way to send a message so they were praying that the father would return in time for the burial.

They could not wait any longer and while they were carrying his body to the place of burial, Joel's father returned, and asked them, "What are you doing?" They replied, "Little Joel died yesterday and we are on the way to bury him." Papa Rameau said, "No! You will not bury him, because God told me that Joel will be a great preacher who will affect all of Haiti!" He stopped the procession and started praying over the little coffin. He was praying about one and a half hours and the people were getting restless. Then they heard a child sneeze but there were no children around. So they opened the coffin and little Joel was alive. This resurrection happened after he was dead nearly 30 hours. Praise God! He is alive and serving Jesus!

When Joel first told me this testimony, immediately I was led to tell Joel, "You must go public with this testimony for the glory of God." So he appeared on the 700 Club with Ben Kinchlow, then with his father on the Richard Roberts Show, and then with Paul and Jan Crouch.

Joel and Doris host a TV show two times a week in Port-au-Prince. They also are on radio that covers most of Haiti. Bishop

Joel was instrumental in breaking the spirit of Voodoo in the land of Haiti.

The home church called Grace Tabernacle has grown to over 4,000 in the two services on Sunday mornings. They have a boys home on the compound. God helped them to build a girls home about two miles from the home base in Lamaten. They have about 60 girls. They also built a large church that will seat about 3,000 people and they have a school on this property.

The Lord has led Bishop Joel to build a children's hospital adjacent to the property. So they sent a letter to Paul and Jan Crouch asking them to pray for this project. Jan was so blessed with this opportunity because the Lord already had put this desire on her heart to help Haiti in this way. So she brought this need on the Praise The Lord television program and the people responded very favorably to meet this need. This 100 bed children's hospital is now being built.

On our last trip there were 800 students at the school and over 250 new churches were planted all over the land of Haiti by the help of Gospel Crusade, Gerald Derstine and Grace Chapel and others throughout the United States and Canada. Joel Jeune is the Bishop of the churches in Haiti and the Haitian Director for Gospel Crusade.

Buying the Land
(As told to me by Bishop Joel Jeune.)

"The miracle of possessing the land where our school is built cannot be put to silence. The property is located right in front of our church. One morning the owner showed up with a group of people to survey the land. He was going to sell it to a nightclub owner. I felt led by the Holy Spirit to go to the owner and talk to him. So I told him that he must sell the land to my church since it was located right next to the church. He got furious at first but after much talk he said that he would give me one week to come up with $5,000 if I wanted to buy the property. I was in so much trouble now

111

because I didn't even have five cents towards buying any land. We went to God in prayer and God sent Papa Luke unexpectedly to Haiti with a gift of $500 for my church and he arrived just one day before our time limit. Early the next morning I took him with me to the owner of the land. After we talked and prayed a few times, Papa Luke took his hand and prayed this time that the owner would accept the $500 as down payment. He reluctantly agreed and we made the rest of the payments until we possessed the land on which our school building is now built. This same building that has been built upon this miraculous gift of God is also being used for children's church, youth activities, seminars and many other purposes. Praise God for his servant!"

The school children in Haiti.

Edna and Josiah giving out pencils.

CHAPTER 19
HOLY LAND VISIT

Where Jesus Walked

I had a desire to see where Jesus was born, where He walked and did His miracles and where He died. I also wanted to visit the empty tomb. This became a reality in November 1968. The first day I said to Edna and my friend, Leo, "It feels like we came home." There was such peace praying at the Wailing Wall now called the Western Wall of the Temple Mount. This place is the most holy place of prayer for the Jewish people. I also put a prayer request on paper and put it in one of the cracks in the wall.

I found great consolation while kneeling at a rock in the Garden of Gethsemane. It was an awesome experience to kneel by an olive tree in the garden that was believed to be 2,000 years old. It could be possible that Jesus prayed at this same place.

Praying at the Western Wall (The Wailing Wall)

When we walked up Mt. Calvary, I wept as I knelt in worship and remembered Jesus' crucifixion. I said to the Lord "Why did You die for me?", and I heard in my spirit Jesus saying "Because I love you." In a new way I was thankful for my salvation and thankful that my name is written in Heaven in the Lamb's Book of Life.

We worshipped our God at Caesarea Philippi where Jesus "asked His disciples, saying unto them, 'Whom do men say that I am?' And they answered, 'John the Baptist: but some say, Elias; and others, One of the prophets.' And He saith unto them, 'But whom say ye that I am?' And Peter answereth and saith unto Him, 'Thou art the Christ,' Mark 8:27-29."

Crossing the Sea of Galilee where Jesus had walked on the water and stopping in the middle of the sea, we had a time of worship. Afterwards we went to the Mount of Beatitudes where Jesus gave His Sermon on the Mount, the greatest sermon ever preached. (Matthew 5, 6 and 7)

While visiting the Dead Sea, I found it very interesting to swim and float there. I was able to read a Voice magazine while floating on the Dead Sea.

In 1973 I took another trip to Israel. Just before our tour group was about to leave for Israel, the Yom Kippur War broke out. Therefore, none of the airlines were permitted to send flights into Israel at this time. However, our tour leader did not take no for an answer. While he had our group of 120 people fly out to Paris, France, where we waited at the international airport all day, he contacted the Israeli travel agent in Israel. This travel agent in turn went to the Minister of Tourism in Jerusalem and asked permission to send one of Israel's El Al airplanes from Tel Aviv to Paris to pick us up. This Minister of Tourism was also a member of Israel's Parliament at that time.

About six o'clock that evening we were able to board the EL AL airplane and fly to Israel. When we arrived in the Holy Land, we had to land in what was total darkness because of a blackout since the war was going on. We were the only tour group in the Holy Land. The war was so tense that President Nixon had to put all of the U.S. military on Alert One. It seemed that we were sent to Israel to pray rather than to just go on a tour. But thank God! He gave them peace.

Edna and me by an old olive tree
(believed to be nearly 2,000 years old)
in the Garden of Gethsemane.

Praying in the Garden of Gethsemane.

CHAPTER 20 - RISE UP AND BUILD

The New Grace Chapel

God used a radio evangelist who said on the radio, "If you send me an offering I will send you a Book of Prophecy by Anna Shrader." I had these books, so I got them out of the closet and placed them on the hassock to look at them. Later on that evening, I sat on my favorite chair and felt that God had a word for me. I picked up the Book of Prophecy given to me by the prophetess sometime earlier. As I turned to the second page, my eyes fell on these words, "I command you to rise up and build." "Edna, I believe I got a word from the Lord!" I read over and over again this word. It got into my spirit. On Sunday morning, I shared this word with the congregation and again on Sunday night.

After service Sunday night, Charles Forney said to me, "Brother Luke, where did you see those mulberry trees?" Now Charles and Sara had been talking to me about how God had revealed to them that we were to build a church on their

Grace Chapel

property. I really was not interested because I thought it was too far from the city of Harrisburg. So I answered that the mulberry trees were an instance in the Bible where God gave Israel direction to go ahead in battle.

Charles saw my disinterest and he hung his head in disappointment. "Charles, do you have any mulberries on the field you were talking to me about?" "Yes," Charles said, "Lots of them." That was a key in the prophecy to get my attention. "I'll be over to see the field tomorrow." I shared my vision with the elders and the board members and together we prayed and believed that this was our direction to build the new Grace Chapel.

While I was away on a ministry trip, the A-frame roof trusses were put in place. My son, Melvin, told me that a white dove sat on one of them. Praise the Lord! We always received this as a blessing of God's Holy Spirit. While we were building the new church facility, a thought of human reasoning came to me, "Why don't you cut back on missions until you get the new building built." I thought just a moment and said "Get out of here, devil. We will double our missions giving when we move into the new building!" And God did it! We went from $26,000 to $52,000 the first year we were in the new building!

On Wednesday night, July 10, 1977, we had our first service in the new Grace Chapel. John Gimenez was the guest speaker. The dedication service was held on July 17, 1977 and Gerald Derstine was our guest speaker. The building was packed out. Friends came from far and near. Prophecies were spoken that God would bless and multiply. Soon Grace Chapel blossomed. The congregation doubled in size twice in two years. God was blessing and pouring out of His Spirit upon us. It was a time of refreshing from the presence of the Lord. Many were saved and backsliders were brought back to the Lord.

At the time of building the gymnasium and the Prayer Garden, I put the names of all of our children and church family as well as many of our friends inside the south wall of the Prayer Garden as a permanent memorial unto the Lord.

Pastor Mel Becomes Senior Pastor

In 1978, Pastor Mel was employed as associate pastor of Grace Chapel. He continued in this capacity, providing assistance in the administration of the church and preaching periodically until the winter of 1985. It was then that I received a word from the Lord that I should step down as senior pastor to give me the time that I need to pursue the missionary vision.

Melvin was eight years old when we moved to Harrisburg. He always wanted to go with me to prayer meetings or visitations. Edna's concern was that he should go to bed earlier so he would do well in school the next day. I said to Edna "Since he has a desire to go with me on ministry, let us allow him to go." The call of God on Melvin's life was noticeable early in his life.

Psalms of David

One of the ministers that came to Grace Chapel was Deck Silverman and his wife. His ministry group was called the Psalms of David. They brought a spirit a revival as they sang and led the congregation in worship. God's presence was so beautiful and the congregation in unison danced before the Lord for a long time. It seemed like the whole building was shaking and we noticed that the whole floor of the church kept moving. Some of the children's workers in the basement became concerned as they saw the basement ceiling moving up and down during this special time of rejoicing in the Lord.

Bob and Jeanie Johnson were another couple who were a great inspiration to us. They held several concerts at Grace Chapel and we were truly blessed to have them minister and sing for us.

CHAPTER 21
GRACE CHAPEL MISSION

World Missions

Shortly after moving into the new building, the first missionary convention was conceived and initiated. That effort has continued with annual missionary conventions. These conventions reflect one central theme of this ministry — World Missions are both local and foreign. There was no doubt that the Grace Chapel missions program had grown. The 1964 budget of $300.00 had grown until, by 1986, $290,487.87 passed through the mission books. From two missionaries supported by Grace Chapel in 1964, the number increased to 32 in 1999. These are signs of lives that have been touched and changed for the Glory of Jesus Christ, and who are committed to the redemptive purposes of God on this earth. Only eternity will reveal the real growth of that part of God's outreach called Grace Chapel as He measures it in terms of His eternal plan and purpose. May we be found faithful.

After All of these Great Blessings

After all of these great blessings and the growth of world and local missions outreach, the enemy of our soul took the occasion to hinder the work. One of the brothers on staff was giving wrong counsel to some of our young people. Contention came into the church and many of the families left. When we finally got proof of this misconduct, we dismissed this brother from his position. Already there was a lot of disunity within the church family. Another member who was a close friend of ours took the occasion and created a lawsuit against me and against the church. This brought a cloud of gloom against me and the church. I struggled with this for possibly nearly two years. One day in a Sunday worship service, I chose to put this offense under the blood forever. I made a strong declaration to God and said, "I choose to forgive this brother even if he never comes and asks me for forgiveness."

Recently I went to Pennsylvania for my uncle's funeral. He was 91 years old and was my last uncle. My friend, Tom Martin, picked me up at the airport. We went to a nearby restaurant for lunch. To my surprise the brother who betrayed me was having lunch with his wife. My first thought was that this will be interesting to see what happens when they pass by us as they leave. My second thought was "I will not wait for that but I will go over and greet them while they are still sitting at the table." I went to them and said to her, "How are you?" and shook her hand. Then I turned to him and said, "How are you, and how is your health?" They both responded by saying that they were fine and that their health was fine.

This was a great blessing to me because this was the first time in seven years that I saw them. I was so happy because there was no resentment or unforgiveness in my heart. Forgiveness is a choice, not a feeling.

The Missionary Trip Around the World

In the mid-80's, Edna and I flew to Amsterdam and spent two days there with Patty Burns and Jeanie Nye. From this place, we went to Bangkok, Thailand and to Shanghai. Afterwards we went to Hong Kong with Brother Thurmond who later took me into mainland China. Then we went to the Philippines and ministered with Brother and Sister Cortez. The next stop was Korea, and we visited Dr. Cho's church and the Prayer Mountain and spent some time in a small prayer room on this mountain. After we crossed the Pacific, we stayed with our daughter, Marty and her family, in Salem, Oregon for four days. Our final four days were spent with our other daughter, Irene, and her family, in Texas.

Our missionary trip around the world took us 34 days. Many of our family members and friends welcomed us home at the Harrisburg International Airport.

We rode an elephant in Thailand.

Our Trip to Africa

On another trip, after we landed in Johannesburg, South Africa and then on to Durban the next day, we flew on to Harare, Zimbabwe to meet with our friends, the Rosells. Gail and Jerry took good care of us. They took us up the Zambezi River to visit the Vandoma Tribe. This was their fourth trip there. We stayed at an old army camp which had been unused and unkept. So we cleaned it up. We had brought our folding cots along. It was so hot that night without any air moving and it seemed like high in the 90's. While we were there, Edna became ill in the night time with some symptom of a heart attack or heart failure. We prayed and confessed any sins we could think of. You see, we were 200 miles from a hospital way back in the bush. At breakfast we shared what had happened last night with our missionary friends and, again, we prayed and God healed Edna. It wasn't until then that we realized what our daughter, Marty, had told us before we went on this trip. She felt that we were to pray the 91st Psalm everyday while we were in Africa. We were so thankful that

God had healed Edna even though we forgot to pray this prayer until after she had gotten sick!

After this, Lester and Peggy Saylor came to Harare and took us to Karaba where they lived. We were there to dedicate their center, "The Most High Hotel." That Sunday morning I called home to Mel and Rosemary to see how everyone was. Rosemary said, "Did you get our telegram?" Luke, Jr. had an accident with the big milk truck. The truck rolled over 4 times and he was unconscious. They had to do an emergency operation on him and found a ruptured spleen. They lost his blood pressure two times during the operation. The hospital called Mel and Earl and said that if they want to see their brother alive, they must come right away. Luke, Jr. was unconscious for 14 hours. As we look back we discovered that the night Edna became sick was the time of the accident and God had us awake and praying because of the pains in her body. God knows all things!

CHAPTER 22
THE PROTECTING ANGELS

My Protecting Angels

Edna and I were traveling from Pennsylvania to Florida and we stayed with Ronald and Pat McEntyre for the night and fellowship. That night, Ron and I were watching the ten o'clock news and I needed to go to the bathroom. As I approached the hall, still looking back to catch the last glimpse of the news I opened the door with my left hand thinking I was stepping into the bathroom. But instead, I found myself starting to fall down the basement steps, with my body at about a 45 degree angle and my left hand slipping off the door knob. I finally stopped in mid air. It was humanly impossible for me to stop that fall, but praise God for His protecting angel that stopped me from falling down the steps. Psalms 34:7 says, "The angel of the Lord encampeth round about them that fear Him, and delivereth them."

Another time I went fishing with Earl and his sons, Nathan and Kevin, at Egmont Key. Now Egmont Key has the remains of an old military fort. Some of us got on the old concrete cannon base about 100 yards out in the water to do some fishing. When it was time to leave, Nathan brought the boat as close as possible to the concrete where I was standing. I was holding the cooler chest and I stepped onto the rocking boat. Kevin took the cooler and at that moment the boat shifted away and I fell backwards into the water. Now my head was so very close to the sharp concrete that it was a miracle that my head missed it. When I hit the water it was such a beautiful experience. My straw hat floated away but I was able to retrieve it.

That night before we retired we were reminiscing about the fishing trip and my fall. All of a sudden, we became aware that it was the protecting angel of the Lord. Isaiah 63:9 says "...the angel of His presence saved them: in His love and in His pity He redeemed them."

Leroy and Fannie Fisher were visiting us from Pennsylvania. Leroy and I went picking oranges at Earl's duplex in Bradenton. I had put the eight foot ladder up against a limb of the orange tree in the backyard. The top end of the ladder was positioned about three inches higher than the limb which went straight out from the tree. I failed to calculate that when I picked the oranges from the tree and put them in my bag, the ladder could sink a bit into the soft sand. All of a sudden to my surprise, the ladder slipped off the tree limb which had moved upward above the ladder after I lifted off the weight of oranges from the limb. While I was standing on the three foot high step, I fell backwards and landed on my back in the yard. Leroy heard the commotion and asked "What's going on?" "Oh, I just fell off the ladder." "Are you hurt?" "No, it felt like I landed on a bed mattress." I believe it was God's protecting angel. Psalms 91: 11-12 says "...for He shall give His angels charge over thee, to keep thee in all thy ways. They shall bear thee up in their hands, lest thou dash thy foot against a stone."

Snow Blizzard

Edna and I went to Pennsylvania by car for the missionary convention. We stayed with Edna's sister, Minerva, on Friday night. A beautiful snow had fallen by morning. The forecaster had predicted the snow blizzard perfectly even though I had been skeptical. We were planning to go fifteen miles east to our friends, Leon and Ruth Hershey. But at the last moment when we left Talmage near Lancaster, we decided to go to Melvin and Rosemary's house in Elizabethtown. The snow had gotten so bad that we barely made it. Both the Interstate and the Pennsylvania Turnpike were officially closed. Everyone was warned to stay home. We were thankful for a warm house and electricity. Edna was so happy that we were snowed in, and it was very interesting to her to see these two preachers snowed in and not able to get to church.

Pastor Phil Derstine was the guest speaker that year. His plane could not land at the Harrisburg Airport because the snow blizzard closed it up. But he was able to land in Allentown and rent a car to drive to Elizabethtown. Now there were three preachers that could not get to church.

It was just before noon on Saturday and while in the heart of this blizzard which was life threatening, I had a concern and a burden for someone that could be caught in this storm. While I was watching the snow through the window and winds blowing up to 70 miles per hour, I prayed for anyone who might be trapped in this blizzard.

The following winter Clarence and Arlene Weaver visited us at Christian Retreat in Florida. They are distant relatives of ours. Arlene told us this incredible story. On the day of the snow blizzard, they had gone to Richland and had a late breakfast with their son Dean. They also were told by radio to stay off the road and stay at home. But like me, they loved snow and Arlene loves driving in the snow. They didn't believe the weather forecaster either. About noon they started for home now realizing the forecasters had predicted this storm perfectly. When they came about a mile and a half near their home, they could not get any further with the car. So they stopped at a neighbor's house. Since the storm was raging, their friend asked them to stay. But Clarence and Arlene felt responsible to get home since they had 60,000 chickens to care for. So reluctantly their friend gave them his four wheel drive jeep. They thought they could make it through the field. However, they didn't get very far before the jeep got stuck in the snow with all four wheels spinning.

Their son, David, said, "If I go this direction, I can find the fence and then follow it to the barn." However, when he got about six feet from the jeep, they saw him fall in the snow. Because the snow was blowing so hard, they could not see him anymore. As Clarence and Arlene waited what seemed like hours, the wind continued to be so strong and loud that they could not talk to each other. The snow was blowing between the curtains of the jeep. Then there was a knock at the door of the jeep. David was there with the big Dueitz

Diesel. The tractor was about ten feet from the car, but they could not see it or hear the sound of the motor. They quickly got out of the jeep and onto the tractor. While on the tractor, Arlene stood on the draw bar and did not have the strength to hold on since it was freezing cold. And just as she was about to fall off, a strong arm came around her and held her securely.

When they came into the house, they fell on the floor from cold and exhaustion. David decided to take a shower to thaw out from the cold. Arlene said to Clarence, "Thank you for holding me so that I wouldn't fall from the tractor." Clarence responded, "I didn't hold you. I was using all my strength to hold myself." So Arlene said to David, "Thank you for holding me from falling off the tractor." But David said "I didn't hold you. I needed both hands to drive the tractor." It was not until then that they thanked God for his protecting angel. Or perhaps it was the fourth man as in Daniel 3:25, "Lo, I see four men loose, walking in the midst of the fire, and they have no hurt; and the form of the fourth is like the son of God."

Pony Cart Accident

A number of years ago, we had a ministers' conference at Grace Chapel and Brother Gerald Derstine spoke on a Sunday night. At the close of the next session on the following Monday morning, one of the ministers, Brother George Cross, said, "Let's pray for our grandchildren's safety and protection." Since he made the request I asked him to lead in prayer. While he was praying, my secretary, Brenda Martin, came to me and said, "Your grandsons, Josiah and Marcus, were in a pony cart accident." I then closed the meeting and went to the scene of the accident. Josiah, who was two and a half years old, was already taken to the hospital while Marcus, three years old, still unconscious, was being worked on by the paramedics. Rosemary, Marcus' mother, was very devastated. She looked at the scripture verse that she had pinned on her blouse that morning. It said that "no weapon formed against you shall prosper" and this gave her courage.

That day, Luke, Jr. had hitched his pony onto the cart and was giving his nephews a ride. Just as Irene was taking a picture, the pony went wild and started to run away. Quickly Luke, Jr. violently pulled on the reins and the one rein broke. So he jumped onto the back of the pony to grab hold of his bridle, but fell off and the pony ran over him. The cart upset and Marcus and Josiah were caught in it and were dragged along on the ground. Marcus' head hit a tree so hard that it knocked him out, and the pony was dragging them across the Nissleys' field. Luke, Jr. and Irene arrived at the farm shortly after the pony had turned around in front of the house and stopped by the front door. He still had about one half mile to go to his stable. We believe that it was an angel of the Lord that stopped the pony. Perhaps this was the same angel that appeared to Luke, Jr. when he was seven years old.

All of Marcus' skin was taken off his back. When Luke, Jr. picked him up it seemed like his skull was crushed and he was not breathing. Mrs. Nissley was at home and they laid Marcus on the couch. Luke, Jr. prayed for Marcus and rebuked death and Marcus started breathing again. The grandsons were both taken to Hershey Medical Center where they applied the placenta of a newborn on Marcus' back. His back was healed without a scar but he has a scar on the back of his head where he hit the tree.

Edna was called at the shopping center to come home because of the emergency. When she got home we joined together in prayer. Edna prayed that the Lord would get these boys out of the hospital in less than a week. After prayer I said to Edna "You don't realize how serious they were injured." Edna said "Well, I already prayed. What shall I do about it?" We took Gerald and Beulah Derstine with us to the hospital to see and pray for the boys. One look at Marcus and Gerald said "You could be making other plans," meaning funeral arrangements. I kept my preaching commitment in New York State the next day and continued contacting home by phone.

On Thursday Edna said "They are coming home from the hospital tomorrow. Is that all right with you?" You see God answered her prayer. I was able to come home one day earlier and we prayed and anointed with oil both Josiah and Marcus at church and asked God to heal both of them without any after effects. Praise God! He answered prayer again!

The Floating Wallet

We had the blessing of going on our first cruise in December 2000. The cruise took us to Mexico, Cozumel and then to the Cayman Islands. There was a group of 50 of our friends with us.

I enjoyed snorkeling with Earl and I took some pictures while under the water. When we got back to land a man said, "Are you Mr. Weaver?" When I acknowledged this, the man handed me my check book and wallet and said, "We found this floating in the water." I was so surprised and thankful. I thanked him again and again. I asked him, "What could I do for you?" He said, "Be nice to Jehovah's Witnesses when they come to your door," and I gladly promised that I would be nice to them.

When Earl and I came to the lounge where Joy was waiting, we told her about this. I realized I had forgotten to take off my bermuda shorts which I wore over my swim suit. I had kept my wallet in the left front pocket. When we went back to our ship, I sat next to the man that found my floating wallet. So I gave him a gift of appreciation for giving everything back to me.

This reminds me of a contact that I had with a Jehovah's Witness many years ago. As we sat in the living room, I asked the young man to tell me his story. After he concluded his witness, I said, "You have one problem. You have a kingdom but you do not have a King." I said this because they do not recognize the blood atonement as being necessary for salvation.

Yes, I was nice to him. You see being nice to people is the only effective way that you can be a witness for our Lord.

CHAPTER 23
OYSTER BAY

Ministry to Long Island

My name was put into Don Basham's book *Deliver Us From Evil* as a reference minister. As a result of the publishing of this book, we received many calls from all over the northeastern part of the country. Trudy Demeo and her sister, Rosemary, came to our house for a weekend for the purpose of receiving deliverance and to learn more about the ways of God.

They both felt the peace of God in our home, and asked us to come and teach their people how to have a Christian home like we have. Trudy was from Oyster Bay, Long Island and Rosemary was from New York City. This contact took us to Oyster Bay many times for ministry. Trudy arranged for a meeting in her home and invited her friends to come to meet with us for personal ministry.

A school teacher came for counseling and ministry. Her burden was for her father's salvation. I asked her if her father was still living and she told me that her father passed away three years ago. I quickly asked the Lord in silence how to help her overcome her burden. God helped me. I said, "Let us put your father into the hands of a just and loving God", and then I had a prayer for her. Both Edna and I saw in her a great big burden lifted off her and we thanked God for His wisdom and blessing.

On another occasion, we were invited to the home of Joan Hayes for a morning meeting. When Joan met us the night before, she was quite skeptical of us country people. But God by His Spirit directed Edna to speak in the meeting that night about the little foxes that destroy the vines. This was the sign to Joan to confirm our coming to her house that next morning. There were 21 people in the meeting and I was a bit nervous about meeting all those people that seemed to be from high class society. However, I opened up the meeting and introduced Edna to them. I did not realize that she had had a similar concern and had already prayed through on this matter. Edna did well and blessed the people with her witness. By that time I had a freedom in my spirit to share the Word and testimonies. I asked how many would like to receive Jesus as their Saviour and all 21 of them raised their hands. I led them in a prayer of commitment to Jesus. Joan had arranged for Edna to be at one end of this mansion and I was put in a lounge at the other end so that each one had personal time with us. Some of them did not have a Bible.

On the way back to Trudy's house, Trudy told us who some of these people were. The lady of the house, Joan Hayes, was the chaplain of Columbia University and was a Spirit-filled believer. One of the ladies in the meeting was the wife of the president of Tele-Star. Another lady was the wife of the president of a large rubber company. Joan's husband, Hank Hayes, was a retired president of the Kennedy Airport and also the president of the Eastern Division of Eastern Airlines.

At another time when we had breakfast with Hank and Joan, I showed interest in his work and asked all kinds of questions about airplanes. When we left that day, Hank walked with us to the car. We were told afterwards that this was the first time he walked any of Joan's Christian friends to the door. Praise God! We touched his heart and were a witness to him.

On a later visit, Joan invited her daughter from California and her son from Denver, Colorado, to fly in and meet us. We were able to be of spiritual strength to her children. They were the ones who helped develop the Celestial Seasonings Herbal Tea.

CHAPTER 24
ACRES OF DIAMONDS

Bloom Where You Are Planted

A classic story was once told about Ala Hofa who sold his property in South Africa for the purpose of searching for diamonds elsewhere so that he could get wealthy. Later on diamonds were discovered on that property. This created the Mangola Diamond Mines while Ala Hofa died in poverty and failure.

One time I cut down a dead tree for firewood and split it up only to discover later that it was black walnut probably worth more than a thousand dollars.

Luke, Jr. was given a mandola, a larger version of a mandolin, as a gift. After he was married he sold it for a few hundred dollars. Later on he discovered that it was worth over $30,000. The factory that manufactured mandolas had burned down in 1929 and they discontinued making them.

Remember! "Bloom where you are planted. God may want to use you and bless you right where you are." (Author unknown)

CHAPTER 25
50TH WEDDING ANNIVERSARY

Comments from the Children

IRENE:

"Marty and Phil took the entire Weaver family to New York City. Daddy was able to keep up with us and I was so proud of him. With ten of us in our little gang hopping in and out of the subway ten or more times pushing the baby in a stroller, Dad went all the way with us. We had a great time and I said, "Thank God my Dad has that much health in his old age!" It was a blessing to me to be with the family visiting New York City. It was the first time we had seen the Statue of Liberty and our children were so blessed to see it."

Irene and her sons.

"You probably know that Daddy and Mother are taking this little anniversary trip to Alaska. They take very few pleasure trips since most of their lives they've taken only ministry trips. They've had many trips to Haiti and about six trips to the Philippines. Now they are going on their 50th wedding anniversary trip to their last and 50th state and I think that's pretty neat. Alaska is the only state in the United States they have not seen. I want to thank all of you that came out and made this a very special day for all of us. God bless you."

ROSEMARY:

"Well, I married into this family in 1968. I met Mel in the Bible College in San Antonio. I met his parents when they came down about a year before we were married. After I graduated from the Bible College, his whole family whom I had not met came to our wedding. After we were married in Colorado, we moved to Pennsylvania."

"I appreciate Mom and Dad Weaver and their witness and testimony. I can always rely on Dad Weaver's prayers. Anytime I had a problem being away from home and my family for so many years it was just wonderful to have Christian in-laws who knew how to pray and support us. I just appreciate everything you represent and the heritage you've given to my husband, and I think the most wonderful thing that really stands out in my mind is the Scripture that says you and your children and your children's children will be serving the Lord. The testimony is that all of your children and grandchildren are serving the Lord and your great grandchildren are being taught the ways of the Lord and I think it's a tremendous testimony. And I am thankful to God for this blessing."

"I praise God for each one that's here tonight and for the

Mel and Rosemary and family.

support you've given to Mom and Dad Weaver and the love you've extended to them as well as to the rest of us as a family. As a daughter-in-law, I appreciate how you've received me. So many people who have gone on to be with the Lord were touched by this couple and their ministry. Because of your witness and your testimony countless people have come to know the Lord and several have been called into full time ministry. Your witness has gone around the world. Because of your testimony, I praise God for the opportunity we have to be a part of this family and their ministry."

MEL:
"Reflecting back on Mother and Dad: Mother, you really are responsible for making us children hard workers. That is something that is a hallmark, and I thank God for that. You know on the farm, they made us work and I praise God for that. I say that as a positive thing because I am thankful today."

IRENE:
"See, a lot of things get done just by a little suggestion. When we moved into the house on 40th Street after it was converted into a duplex, the rent on our home was $20 a month. Of course it didn't have inside facilities so you can't charge too much. We lived there eleven years. The rent never went up. Later on the people on the other side moved out. The landlord knew that someday this duplex was going to be torn down so he didn't want to rent it again. We went to him and said 'We need a bigger house, how much would you rent the other side to us?' He said 'You can have the whole house. Your rent won't go up.' So we had the whole sixteen rooms for $20 a month. We needed access to the other side so we needed those walls to be knocked down and Mom said 'Luke, we need a doorway going into those other rooms into the house.' But Dad was a very busy man raising us five kids. One day mother thought she waited long enough so she took the ax and started hacking and making holes in the walls. Then Dad

134

had to do something about that."

"This house then became so big after Dad finished making the doorway. We had so many people during that time. We had a Full Gospel Business Men's convention in Harrisburg and two people who were talking said 'Where are you staying?' 'At the Weaver's.' 'You mean Luke Weaver's?' 'Yes.' 'Well, we're staying there, too.' But they never did meet each other at the house."

MEL:

"That was exciting just to be able to grow up in a family that really was taught good work ethics. Mom and Dad love people. They are there to help us become all that God wants us to be and we thank God for this. We appreciate the man of God that Marcus is. We believe that our children carry on the Godly influence that Mom and Dad gave to us. Marcus is [1995] working at a farm owned by a dentist nearby and his wife said in a birthday card that she appreciates his Godly example and hopes he always keeps it up. And Dad, I just am thankful how you showed us what a real man of God is."

EARL:

"Well, it's good to be here. It's been quite a day seeing so many friends. I'm thankful for the precious memories we have and for being taught in the ways of the Lord. Mom had different punishments for us kids. One of them was washing dishes. I remember washing dishes standing on a little bench so I could reach the spigot. If you did something wrong you got a week's worth of chores to do. It's just great being a family and just having a lot of good memories growing up together like building a pony shed for Luke, Jr. for the little pony he had and taking care of the homing pigeons and rabbits and normal things a country bumpkin would have."

"We count it a privilege to live in Florida with Mom and Dad. They live at Christian Retreat and we live sixteen miles away in Bradenton."

Earl and Joy and family.

JOY:

"I don't know whether I can [speak] or not. It hasn't hit me yet until right now. Looking out over this congregation, as Earl said, reminds me of so many memories of so many wonderful times. I come from a family of three. So when I married into this clan, it was a real culture shock, being an only child. But the Lord knew what we needed to balance our lives out. He knew I needed big sisters and brothers and an extended family and that's what you all are. And I want to thank Mom and Dad Weaver for the many times they've prayed for Earl and me, our three children, and for this church and for the times they kept the doors open and the times they cried in the middle of the night when nobody knew it and the heartaches that were on their hearts because Grace Chapel is their baby also. This baby has grown and matured and is still growing and still strong and will continue to grow long after all of us have gone. Tonight we give you honor and we know it's the Jesus inside you that's kept you going and by the grace of God we're going to follow in your footsteps."

NATHAN:

"It's been fabulous having grandparents like Grandpa and Grandma Weaver. Now that I am married to Erica, I see the great example that they have set for all of us as far as communications go between you two being able to work together and the constant effort you have put forth in order to make everything work out. And I couldn't ask for better grandparents than what I've got and I want to say thank you."

MARTY:

"I want to thank all of you for coming out to join in the special celebration day for Mom and Dad. It's a real joy to see so many people that I haven't seen for years and I count it a privilege just to be here for this big reunion. We live in Salem, Oregon."

Marty and Phil and family.

"Phil was going to Elim Bible Institute and during his senior year they sent him into different ministers' homes for a week of practical ministry. And so he was in our home for a week. In the daytime he'd go with Dad on ministry outreach and visitation and then in the night Dad would say 'OK girls, why don't you take him places and do things with him.' The School had real strict dating policies at Elim Bible Institute but as Phil was getting in the car to come to our home for that week of practical ministry, Brother Johannson, who was the dean of men, said 'Oh, by the way I bet you didn't know this, but there are five nurses living in the Weaver's basement' and Phil said 'I bet you've been dying to tell me that!' Irene and I were going through nurses' training at the time and we had three nursing students who were also living with us during the week at the time. We had a little apartment down there. We had a lot of fun together. Phil was real practical and that same year we were married. The Lord blessed us with four beautiful children."

"Special Word of Encouragement – This is the word of the Lord for Mom and Dad."

"I love you! You are so very special to Me! You are the apple of My eye. Before the foundation of the world, I knew you and started planning ahead and making provision for all you ever needed and are going to need. My resources are limitless and My storehouses are always full."

"Don't ever think I have not heard your prayers. I have nestled every word in My tender loving care and even the smallest details are important to Me."

"The dark pieces of the puzzle that are falling into place right now are just shadows in a beautiful picture. Remember, the brighter the sunlight, the darker the shadows. You cannot even fathom the beauty of your life's picture I am in the making of, even now. Even before the puzzle picture is complete, as each new piece is added, not only you but many around you will and are being blessed to be able to partake of the beauty in even the partial picture."

"Immediately after a rose or flower is crushed, is the greatest fragrance."

"Trust Me! I do know what I'm doing or allowing in your life right now and I have already made full provision for all you need to go through these circumstances victoriously. You're not alone! I will never leave you or forsake you. I am not through using you yet. We're partners and joint heirs. The authority that I have is within you! You're bought with a price and you are precious to Me and always will be."

"Come, take My hand, walk with Me and you'll never again need to question the direction in your life. I desire your communion and fellowship. I long for you just to be with Me. You are My handiwork, a real work of art. All those around you will bask in My beauty as you stay close to Me!"

"God Bless you, Mom and Dad."

PHIL:

"I was just reminiscing and thinking back on some of the things over the years. Marty had mentioned that I was a student at Elim and had spent a week with the pastors. I had never been with a man who was so much on the go in all of my life. This man had so much energy and was so generous to people. It just amazed me. It left an impression on my life that I have never forgotten. It's been a constant challenge to me."

"Mel had mentioned something about Mom and her drive. During that week I was doing some repair work underneath Dad's car and Mom came out on the porch to talk to me. I was interested in Marty but I didn't think anything could develop between us just by being down here for one week since I would be going back to New York. So I just kind of put it aside. Well, Mom came out and got real practical talking with me about Marty's feelings toward me. So I got the inside scoop and so it was later on that week that Marty and I got together and I thank you, Mom, for that. Amen!"

LUKE, JR.:

"I'm honored to be standing before a group of people that have done so much in supporting Dad and Mom, and also us as little Weaver children."

"Some years ago we moved to Canada to pastor a church. Bonnie's home is in Canada. After we had moved there, I met this lady who came to me after a meeting and she said 'Is your Dad's name Luke Weaver?' And I said 'Yes.' And she said 'I prayed for you back years ago when you were going through a lot of hard times in your life.' She said she was a friend of my Aunt Alta's, who was part of Transport for Christ, and they used to pray for the little preacher's kid who wasn't what a preacher's kid ought to be."

"I appreciate each one of you that gave up your time sacrificially to come here and honor Dad and Mom this evening and I want to thank you first hand for your prayers for the children of Mom and Dad and namely for myself. I appreciate your prayers. It seemed that the other children stayed on track pretty well, but I had a need of your prayers to bring me back on track and I thank you for your having a part in the ministry of Dad and Mom. I was blessed with a family, Bonnie, my wife, and Lisa, my daughter."

Luke, Jr. and Bonnie and their girls.

"After we lived in Canada for five years and after Lisa was born, we were expecting another baby who was Luke Justin. However, we lost him going on into the eighth month of pregnancy last February. Being 40 years old at the time we thought that was old enough not to have any more children but the doctor encouraged us to try for another child. We never expected that God would double the blessings back to us. In September she went in for an ultrasound and afterwards she called and said 'We're having twins.'"

BONNIE:
"Our little boy died the eighth day of February and the ground was so cold. Since there was so much snow and everything was frozen, we had to wait until spring when the ground thawed before we could even bury him. Mom and Dad Weaver came up for the funeral which was only a small committal service. We walked behind the church to the grave site. Normally the grave is all dug out with the little white casket sitting there waiting for the undertaker to lower it down

into the ground and we would walk away leaving the rest of the burial procedures to be handled by the undertaker. But Dad and Luke, Jr. each took a shovel [according to an old Mennonite tradition] and began to throw the dirt onto the little white casket [until they completely covered the grave.] I remember as I was standing there on that hillside with the wind blowing on my face, the Spirit of God spoke to my heart and said 'You're burying one seed but you're carrying another.' This took place in May and I had no idea I was pregnant. Of course, I went to Walmart the next day and got a home pregnancy test. The test result was positive. God is good!"

CHAPTER 26
A WORD FROM THE LORD FOR YOU

The Promises of God

Deuteronomy 33:27 "The Eternal God is your refuge, and underneath are the everlasting arms." NKJ

John 14:27 "Peace I leave with you, My peace I give to you; not as the world gives do I give to you. Let not your heart be troubled, neither let it be afraid." NKJ

Isaiah 32:17 &18 "The work of righteousness will be peace, and the effect of righteousness, quietness and assurance forever. My people will dwell in a peaceful habitation, in secure dwellings, and in quiet resting places." NKJ

Romans 15:13 "Now may the God of hope fill you with all joy and peace in believing, that you may abound in hope by the power of the Holy Spirit." NKJ

Hebrews 10:19 & 20 "And so dear brothers and sisters, we can boldly enter heaven's most holy place because of the blood of Jesus. This is the new, life-giving way that Christ has opened up for us through the sacred curtains by means of His death for us." NLT

Matthew 9:37 & 38 "Jesus said to His disciples, the harvest is so great, but the workers are so few. So pray to the Lord who is in charge of the harvest, ask Him to send out more workers for His fields." NLT

Our desire and prayer is that God's hand will be upon many to help bring in the Lord's harvest. I Chronicles 4:10 says "And Jabez called on the God of Israel saying, 'Oh, that You would bless me indeed, and enlarge my territory, that Your hand would be with me, and that You would keep me from evil, that I may not cause pain!' So God granted him what he requested." NKJ

Overcoming Depression

Depression is a problem with many people of all ages.

Personally, this is what has helped me and I used the following scriptures to overcome depression. Luke 22:44 "And being in an agony He prayed more earnestly: and His sweat was as it were great drops of blood falling down to the ground." When Jesus was carrying our sins to the cross, He was also carrying our depressions so that we need not carry our sins and oppressions and so that we can be free. Isaiah 53:7 says that "He was oppressed, and He was afflicted." Isaiah 54:14 tells us that "in righteousness you shall be established; you shall be far from oppression, for you shall not fear; and from terror, for it shall not come near you." NKJ In Acts 10:38 we read "how God anointed Jesus of Nazareth with the Holy Ghost and with power: who went about doing good, and healing all that were oppressed of the devil; for God was with Him."

Seed Time and Harvest

Growing up on the farm, I was taught the value of seed time and harvest. In Genesis 8:22 "While the earth remaineth, seed time and harvest, and cold and heat, and summer and winter, and day and night shall not cease." Our life is a result of seed time and harvest. In Galatians 6:7-9 "Be not deceived: God is not mocked: for whatsover a man soweth, that shall he also reap. For he that soweth to his flesh shall of the flesh reap corruption; but he that soweth to the Spirit shall of the Spirit reap life everlasting. And let us not be weary in well doing: for in due season we shall reap, if we faint not." Every person is into sowing and reaping. I pray that God will help us to sow to the things of the Spirit, and not to the flesh.

Sow a smile and reap many smiles.

Sow a frown and you reap many frowns.

Sow a thought, reap a word.

Sow a word, reap a deed.

Sow a deed, and reap a character.

Sow a character and reap a destiny.

(Some of these thoughts are mine and the rest came from other people.)

When I was a boy they did not have hybrid seeds. So my Dad took the best of the ears of corn from the harvest to plant the next year's corn. I enjoyed counting the seeds on those big ears of corn. There were well over one thousand kernels on an ear of corn. So every kernel of corn had the potential to reproduce itself one thousand times. Jesus said in Matthew 13:23 "But he that received seed into the good ground is he that heareth the word, and understandeth it: which also beareth fruit, and bringeth forth, some an hundredfold, some sixty, some thirty." He also said in Luke 8:15 "But that on the good ground are they, which in an honest and good heart, having heard the word, keep it, and bring forth fruit with patience." In the New Living Translation, this verse reads "But the good soil represents honest, good-hearted people who hear God's message, cling to it, and steadily produce a huge harvest." There is a line from an old church song, "Bringing In The Sheaves," that reads "Sowing in the morning, Sowing seeds of kindness." If we sow seeds of kindness, we will reap a harvest of kindness. Jesus said in Matthew 5:7 "Blessed are the merciful: for they shall obtain mercy."

II Corinthians 9:7-11 says "Every man according as he purposeth in his heart, so let him give; not grudgingly, or of necessity: for God loveth a cheerful giver. And God is able to make all grace abound toward you; that ye, always having all sufficiency in all things, may abound to every good work: (As it is written, He hath dispersed abroad; he hath given to the poor: his righteousness remaineth for ever. Now he that ministereth seed to the sower both minister bread for your food, and multiply your seed sown, and increase the fruits of your righteousness:) Being enriched in every thing to all bountifulness, which causeth through us thanksgiving to God."

If you want a harvest you must put seed in the ground. For most of the Old Testament feasts, the people were expected to bring an offering such as a peace offering and a freewill offering and a thanksgiving offering "at your own will."

(Leviticus 22:21 & 29) The person that did not have peace brought a peace offering. We understand from this that we can name our offering. My first 30 years on the farm, we never planted a seed without a name.

Sometime ago I was encouraging the people to name their seed offering. For instance, if you have a wayward child, plant a seed, and name that seed, "My son or daughter shall come to the Lord." If you need a job or a better paying job, plant a seed with that name. If you have a financial need, plant a seed that God will meet your financial need.

Remember if you want a harvest you must put seed in the ground. Someone in the church planted a seed and named it, "I want to hear from my son," whom they had not heard from for many years. Within ten days that son contacted home! Praise God!

I needed a better car. My old one was over ten years old and I do a lot of driving. So I started to sow seeds for a better car. I wrote on my offering check, "A seed for a late model car." I repeated this many times. You see many seeds are small and a seed offering can be small also. Praise God a three year old late model car was given to me. Then a year later I was told to give this car to my son and the Lord gave me a brand new one, for which I am so thankful. If you are sick, sow a seed for your healing. If you don't have peace with someone, sow a seed for peace as in Leviticus 22:21.

In Malachi 3:7-12 we read "Even from the days of your fathers ye are gone away from mine ordinances, and have not kept them. Return unto me, and I will return unto you, saith the Lord of hosts. But ye said, Wherein shall we return? Will a man rob God? Yet ye have robbed Me. But ye say, Wherein have we robbed Thee? In tithes and offerings. Ye are cursed with a curse: for ye have robbed Me, even this whole nation. Bring ye all the tithes into the storehouse, that there may be meat in Mine house, and prove Me now herewith, saith the Lord of hosts, if I will not open you the windows of heaven, and pour you out a blessing, that there shall not be room enough to receive it. And I will rebuke the devourer for your sakes, and he shall not destroy the fruits of your ground; neither shall your vine cast her fruit before the time in the field, saith the Lord of hosts. And all nations shall call you blessed: for ye shall be a delightsome land, saith the Lord of hosts."

Malachi 3:10 "The windows of heaven" is God's provision. Your human mind quickened by the Spirit of God:

1) It will increase your fruits of righteousness.
   (I Corinthians 9:10)
2) It helps you to make proper financial decisions.
3) It helps you to be in favor with people.
4) The devourer who steals is rebuked. Financial adversity is rebuked; accidents and unnecessary doctor bills and breakdowns are avoided.

The paying of your tithes is a powerful tool for you and God. It puts you into a position where God can bless you.

Giving

As you start your giving by the seed of tithing, the God of Abraham will bless you. Tithing is not a New Testament law, but is confirmed by Jesus in Matthew 23:23(c) "These you ought to have done, without leaving the others undone." NKJ According to Galatians 3:13-14, Christ has redeemed you from the curse of the law so that the blessing of Abraham will rest upon you. The blessings of the law are found in Deuteronomy 28:1-15 as follows:

"And it shall come to pass, if thou shalt hearken diligently unto the voice of the Lord thy God, to observe and to do all His commandments which I command thee this day, that the Lord thy God will set thee on high above all nations of the earth: And all these blessings shall come on thee, and overtake thee, if thou shalt hearken unto the voice of the Lord thy God. 'Blessed shalt thou be in the city, and blessed shalt thou be in the field. Blessed shall be the fruit of thy body, and the fruit of thy ground, and the fruit of thy cattle, the increase of the kine, and the flocks of thy sheep. Blessed shall be thy basket and thy store. Blessed shalt thou be when thou comest in, and blessed shalt thou be when thou goest out.' The Lord shall cause thine enemies that rise up against thee to be smitten before thy face: they shall come out against thee one way, and flee before thee seven ways. The Lord shall command the blessing upon thee in thy storehouses, and in all that thou settest thine hand unto; and He shall bless thee in the land which the Lord thy God giveth thee. The Lord shall establish thee a holy people unto Himself, as He hath sworn unto thee, if thou shalt keep the commandments of the Lord thy God, and walk in His ways. And all the people of the earth shall see that thou art called by the name of the Lord; and they shall be afraid of thee. And the Lord shall make thee plenteous in goods, in the fruit of thy body, and in the fruit of thy cattle, and in the fruit of thy ground, in the land which the Lord sware unto thy fathers to give thee. The Lord shall open unto thee His good treasure, the heaven to give the rain unto thy land in His season, and to bless all the work of thine hand: and thou shalt lend unto many nations, and thou shalt not borrow. And the Lord shall make thee the head, and not the tail; and thou shalt be above only, and thou shalt not be beneath; if that thou hearken unto the commandments of the Lord thy God, which I command thee this day, to observe and to do them: And thou shalt not go aside from any of the words which I command thee this day, to the right hand, or to the left, to go after other gods to serve them. But it shall come to pass, if thou wilt not hearken unto the voice of the Lord thy God, to observe to do all His commandments and His statutes which I command thee this day; that all these curses shall come upon thee, and overtake thee."

The curses of the law are found in the remainder of Deuteronomy chapter 28, verses 15 through 68. If you want to see what our precious Lord Jesus Christ has delivered you from, read the rest of this chapter. So I encourage you to sow for a good harvest by giving and doing deeds of kindness and by your life style.

I Corinthians 15:46 explains that first the natural must occur, then the spiritual. When a seed is planted in the natural, a miracle happens. The seed germinates. The old seed dies and a new plant like it grows up. Many more will come from it when we sow seeds. It is a natural thing that we sow before we reap a spiritual thing which is God's provision and blessings.

"The Road Map to Holiness" By Edna Weaver
(This is Edna's second tract.)

We are all traveling on the highway of holiness which will lead us through this earth to our heavenly home. This road is not always smooth and it has many exits which do lead into the things that could sidetrack us that look ever so good and exciting. Soon we will discover peace has left us if we get off the highway of holiness. There will always be a place to turn around. The Lord our God has given us a road map which is the Bible. So it is always good to start every day looking at the map to be sure you will stay on the highway to holiness. It is always good to remember that Jesus is with us to help us and that He has made a way. Sometimes it looks like this road has taken us into a mud hole, and it looks like we cannot make it, but Jesus is saying to us, "You can make it!"

Many people will be tempted to turn off this exit because the turn off looks smoother. The still small voice of Jesus will be saying, "Don't turn off, there is much more danger in that road, for Satan is on that road trying to get you into his trap." You will find out these side roads are always much more dangerous and have many more heartaches. So always keep God's road map with you and don't forget to read God's road map carefully and know that Jesus is with you wherever you are, holding you in His arms through every rough place. If you can relax and do not struggle out of His hands, you will not get hurt, for He has put a shield around you to protect you, so that even no dart of the enemy can hurt you.

Christ is in you and around you. He is saying, "I will make a way for you where there is no way. 'I am the way, the truth, and the life.'" (John 14:6) NKJ Yes, sometimes on this road, it looks ever so dark. That is the earthly plain you are seeing. But turn your eyes on the heavenly and don't forget that Jesus said, "I am the light of the world" and this light will dispel the darkness. Oh! the light of the glory of His unveiled face is the glory that is changing you and me. He is always with you and He will strengthen you. Nothing can touch you without your Father's promise, not to be tested above what you are able to bear, for He is with you, and He will carry your load, if you let Him. "Trust in the Lord with all your heart; and lean not unto your own understanding." (Proverbs 3:5) Isaiah 55:9 declares that His ways are higher than our ways! His yoke is easy and His burden is light, according to Matthew 11:30.

"I have formed you, Oh, my child. Fear not, for I have redeemed you. You are Mine! I have called you by your name. When you pass through the waters, I will be with you. And through the rivers, they shall not overflow you. When you walk through fire, you will not be burned. Nor shall the flame scorch you. For I am the Lord your God. The Holy One of Israel, your Saviour...Since you are precious in my sight, you have been honored, and I have loved you. Therefore I will give men for you and people for your life. Fear not, for I am with you, I will bring many people in your path...I will bring my sons from afar and daughters from the ends of the earth." (Isaiah 43:l-6) "Do not hold back for I, the Lord, will do this through you, my child. Do not say, 'I can't do that.' I would say, 'I know, that is why I can do it through you.' Too many of My children are doing it in their own strength. They are the ones who will take the glory for themselves. That is why I must stand back and wait until they see the anointing of the Lord leave them, and then they will call on Me. And I am always there for them, and that is when I rejoice that they see 'I am the Lord, that is My name, and I will not give my glory to another.'" (Isaiah 42:8-9) "I will do a new thing for you! So, open your spiritual ears and I will tell you things that are coming your way, then you will be prepared and you will see Me at work through you!" That is why I can say, "If someone would tell you today what the Lord your God has ahead for you, you could not believe it!" The natural man cannot receive the things of God! "Do not remember the former things, nor consider the things of old. Behold, I will do a new thing. Now it shall spring forth. Shall you not know it? I will even make a road in the wilderness and rivers in the desert." I will "give drink to My people, My chosen ones. This My people I have formed for Myself. They shall declare My praise." (Isaiah 43:18-21) NKJ

It will not be as much in what you say as it will be your life, which is Christ in you, the hope of glory, for Jesus is light and in Him is no darkness at all. (I John 1:5) Therefore, see to it that your vessel is not filled up with the things of this world in order that the light of Jesus in your heart may shine through you and the people of this world will see this light of Jesus. (Matthew 5:16) This light is what will draw them to you! It will be the glory of the Lord that will change them. II Chronicles 16:9 declares that "the eyes of the Lord our God run to and fro throughout the whole earth" to find the ones that will release the Christ from within them, so that the glory of the Lord can be seen around them. This happened to Charles Finney. He walked through factories and streets and many people fell down on their faces and gave their hearts to Jesus! These are some of the things that we will see happen as we are willing to pay the price. Salvation is free but being a disciple for Jesus has a price tag on it. No more I but Christ living through me.

The first step to know Jesus is to open your heart and ask Him to come into your life and take over.

Romans 10:13 "For whoever calls upon the name of the Lord shall be saved." NKJ

Romans 10:9 "If you confess with your mouth the Lord Jesus and believe in your heart that God has raised Jesus from the dead, you will be saved." NKJ

John 14:14 "If you ask anything in My name, I will do it." NKJ
John 15:11 "These things I have spoken to you, that My joy may remain in you, and that your joy may be full." NKJ

CHAPTER 27 - CONCLUSION

He Laid His Hand Upon Me

It is with precious memories that I reminisce through life and remember the blessings and victories and the trials where the Lord was with us every time. As in Romans 8:28 "And we know that all things work together for good to them that love God, to them that are the called according to His purpose", we are thankful that we can report that the blessings have far exceeded the trials in life.

I know that the hand of the Lord was upon me when I nearly died at the age of four. I know that God's hand was upon me when I accidentally shot through my foot. His hand was on me when I met this beautiful blue eyed fourteen year old Edna Mae. His hand was on me when I was preaching in the corn field on the new Farmall Tractor. His hand was on me when I for the first time heard the gospel and understood it and became a believer. His hand was on me when Edna and I got married. His hand was on me when God spoke to me about giving up tobacco farming. His hand was on me while I was on my tractor seven years later in June 1955 when the word of the Lord came to me saying, "Leave the farm and go into mission work." His hand was on us when He closed the door on New York City and took us to Harrisburg, Pennsylvania. He laid His hand upon me when I received the Holy Spirit baptism in the old house on 40th Street. His hand was upon us when we started the mission church in Steelton. His hand was on us when we moved the church into the storefront building on Derry Street. His hand was on us to build the new Grace Chapel on Colebrook Road in Elizabethtown. His hand was on me to make many missionary trips around the world.

When God spoke to me in the field to "leave the farm and go into mission work," I never dreamed where He would lead and take me. By the grace of God I traveled into 37 nations of the world and preached in 27 of them. We are planning our 33rd trip into Haiti in November of 2001. So always remember when you go through testing and trials, God's hand is upon you to lead you into the path that He has prepared for you before the foundation of the world. As a believer in our Lord Jesus, His hand is upon you, and God's eternal purposes are being established in your life.

"The chief end of man is to know Him, to serve Him, to love Him and enjoy Him forever." This quote came from an ancient catechism. Numbers 6:24 - 26 says "The Lord bless you and keep you; the Lord make His face shine upon you, and be gracious unto you; the Lord lift up His countenance upon you, and give you peace." NKJ

      With Blessings,
      Pastor Luke and Edna Weaver